TROPHY BASS

An Angler's Guide

by Larry Larsen

Book VII in the Bass Series Library

A LARSEN'S OUTDOOR PUBLISHING BOOK
THE ROWMAN & LITTLEFIELD PUBLISHING GROUP, INC.
Lanham • Chicago • New York • Toronto • Plymouth, UK

Published by
LARSEN'S OUTDOOR PUBLISHING
An imprint of The Rowman & Littlefield Publishing Group, Inc.
4501 Forbes Boulevard, Suite 200, Lanham, Maryland 20706
http://www.rlpgtrade.com

Estover Road, Plymouth PL6 7PY, United Kingdom

Distributed by National Book Network

British Library Cataloguing in Publication Information Available

Library of Congress Cataloging-in-Publication Data Available

Library of Congress 89-92683

ISBN: 978-0-936513-06-5 (paper : alk.paper)

♾™ The paper used in this publication meets the minimum
requirements of American National Standard for Information
Sciences—Permanence of Paper for Printed Library Materials,
ANSI/NISO Z39.48-1992.

Printed in the United States of America

DEDICATION

To the Larsen family for the good times on the banks of the smallest creek to the largest lakes. From the early days of chasing big fish with cane pole and trotline to the more sophisticated means of today, I've enjoyed the numerous angling activities with all my relatives.

ACKNOWLEDGMENTS

My appreciation goes to the thousands of loyal readers of my magazine articles, and most importantly, of my BASS SERIES LIBRARY. Without their support, this continuation of the series of eight books would not be possible. Those that have an understanding of the value of more bass fishing knowledge are my kind of people. They are the better informed and the better anglers. I thank each of you, and will endeavor to provide additional books in this series for interested anglers.

Thanks also to the bass fishermen everywhere that chase lunker bass and release the majority of what they catch. Without such an interest in chasing trophy bass and in their future, our sport wouldn't be gaining in popularity today. Thanks to the big bass chasers and those that want to be more successful catching the trophies. I very much appreciate the innovative and progressive management practices in many states that has led to their having a trophy bass fishery that in a few short years rivals states with overly-conservative attitudes towards developing a strong trophy fishery.

The valuable assistance of my wife, Lilliam, in layout and production of this book is much appreciated. Her diligent copy editing and proofing skills help minimize the mistakes within and make this effort more fun. I also wish to again thank Horace Carter, outdoor writer and book publisher, who helped me get started in book publishing endeavors. His guidance in the "early years" that helped me to establish a foundation of knowledge on book production is appreciated.

PREFACE

"Trophy Bass - An Angler's Guide" is focused at today's dedicated lunker hunters and those that find more enjoyment in wrestling with one or two monster largemouth each day than in horsing a "panfull" of yearlings to the boat. This book takes a look at the geographical areas and waters that might offer better opportunities to catch a giant bass and at successful, proven ways to tempt one. It attempts to explain reasons for geographic production capabilities and explore in some depth what some fishery agencies are doing to emphasize and/or research the trophy bass fishery.

To help the reader better understand how to catch big bass, a majority of this book explores productive techniques for trophies. The information is aimed at those fishermen eager to know more about catching large fish on a less-random basis. Much of the geographic material is based on studies and research projects, while the "how-to" information was gleaned from personal experience, professional guides and other experienced trophy bass hunters. Knowing the ways of the successful big bass anglers should help all anglers be more productive.

This book explores specific catches of true giants in various parts of the country. It examines the "whys" of many catches, as well as the "whens." It discusses the possibilities that our lunker resource is declining and possible steps to turn around such a trend. The common mistakes that cause anglers to lose big fish and the catch-and-release philosophy are also discussed within these covers. The information in "Trophy Bass - An Angler's Guide" should make for productive trophy fishermen, regardless of where they live or their skill level.

CONTENTS

Section Two
TECHNIQUES FOR TROPHIES

ABOUT THE AUTHOR

Larry Larsen is a fisherman/writer who has developed a love for bass fishing. He especially enjoys catching and releasing big bass. He has been fortunate enough to tally almost 200 largemouth between five and 13 pounds, but the true giants that boast outlandish girth and length measurements are still catches in his dreams. He has had two friends lip 15 pound largemouth into his boat, but he is still waiting for such an exciting event. His angling experience is extensive and includes use of artificials and live bait for trophy catches. Larsen has guided two other friends (and himself) to line class world records on the rare (and diminutive) Suwannee bass, but his daily focus is usually on a giant largemouth.

For more than 18 years, Larry Larsen has studied and written about all aspects of bass fishing. He believes in explaining to readers the latest and very best tactics to find and catch bass anywhere. His numerous feature articles in major outdoor magazines and his previously published books in the Bass Series Library detail highly productive fish catching methods and special techniques. In "Trophy Bass," that trend continues.

The author is a frequent contributor on bass subjects to Outdoor Life, Sports Afield, Field & Stream, Bassin', Petersen's Fishing, North American Fisherman, Bass Fishing, Bassmaster, Fishing Facts, and other major outdoor magazines. He has won numerous national awards for his bass fishing articles and photography. His photos have appeared on the covers of many national publications and in countless brochures and advertisements. Larsen is a member of the Outdoor Writers Association of America (OWAA), the Florida Outdoor Writers Association (FOWA), and the Southeastern Outdoor Press Association (SEOPA).

INTRODUCTION

KNOWLEDGE OF THE TROPHY

The Geography Of A Big Bass

PRODUCTIVE TROPHY BASS anglers are usually those who understand the special environmental needs of the giants. They utilize their knowledge of that and current conditions to determine where the trophy largemouth will most likely be located and how they can most effectively catch that fish. By employing the right bait or lure and the best method, an angler fishing the most appropriate area in a good big bass lake will catch one.

Each year, trophy bass specialists assault state records and focus on George Perry's 22-pound 4-ounce world standard bearer. That record remains unchanged, but more than a small armada of bass boats are being launched in search of the most sought-after of all marks.

Anglers in the sunbelt probably would have the best chance of topping the ultimate largemouth record, but others in cooler climates are making strides toward a 22-pound bass. As the trophy fishermen become more conservation-minded and release their big fish, that mark becomes more realistic in many areas.

The very biggest largemouth bass are typically caught in California, Florida, Georgia and Texas. The states are separated distinctly by geography, but a chart of all states that have produced largemouth weighing more than 16 pounds also includes Virginia, Alabama, Arkansas and South Carolina. The southern states big bass production is not too surprising, but Virginia? Consider that a 16-pounder set the Virginia record in 1984, and that it was bested in the spring of 1985.

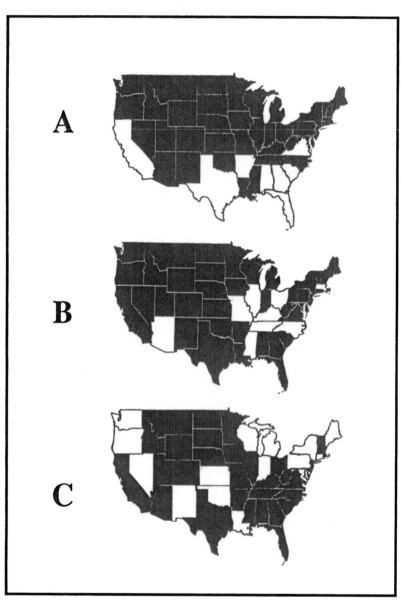

The states with record bass exceeding 16 pounds are shown in A. Those states with records between 13 and 16 pounds are shown in B., while map C indicates states having records between 11 and 13 pounds.

How many states have produced bass over 13 pounds? The answer might surprise you. The chart with standard bearers between 13 and 16 pounds includes nine states. Add that to the eight that have yielded the monsters over 16, and you have 17 states and thousands of waters that have potential for putting a big smile on your face.

Come to think of it, I'm extremely happy with an 11 pounder, and as the chart shows, another 15 states have produced bass that size or greater. The other 18 states in this United States had better have great numbers of 5 and 6 pounders, or they won't see me.

For a complete report on the state marks around the country, turn to the Appendix. The state-by-state listing will be current probably only for a couple of months. Each spring, one or two giants top the mark in one state or another.

"Trophy Bass" has been written as an angler's guide to the geographic "distribution" of huge largemouth, the reasons for a specific area's production and the most successful means of catching a trophy. The book discusses the big bass states of Florida, California and Texas, some of the significant catches and trophy waters. It takes a look at Alabama, Georgia and South Carolina, the "southern belles" of big bass, and details some giants of numerous other states and areas around the country. The geographic explanations are the focus of the five initial chapters. In Chapters 6 and 7, the disappearing giants and those bred through genetic programs are explored.

Chapters 8 through 16 present Techniques For Trophies, those methods and baits that have proven successful for certain habitat and conditions. Natural signs that are keys to big bass locations are analyzed, and specific trophy largemouth methods for use in deep water, after the sun goes down and in moving waters are revealed. Chapters on top water ploys, crankbaiting strategies and flippin' techniques for giants are explored. Pulling huge bass from surface vegetation and using the giant killers - native shiners - are the focus of chapters.

Why big fish get away in Chapter 17 discusses the mistakes that are too common among anglers that are fortunate to have a tussle with a trophy. The book's last chapter presents one man's philosophy of catch and release. It is one the author agrees with, wholeheartedly.

Section One

BIG BASS GEOGRAPHY

- Florida Sunshine

- California Dreaming

- Texas Crude

- Southern Belles

- Worldly Lunkers

- Disappearing Trophies

- Genetic Giants

1 FLORIDA SUNSHINE

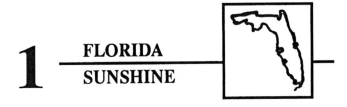

Big Bass Are The State's Biggest Draw

EACH YEAR, FLORIDA waters produce hundreds of ten-pound plus bigmouth. Many of the largest fisheries yield numerous trophy fish and even some of the smaller ones are known for their "wallboard" bass. Any rundown would undoubtedly overlook several good waters with an excellent chance of producing a real monster. To achieve comprehensive coverage of all state lakes that might produce a huge bass would require additional books.

Florida undoubtedly produces more bass over 10 pounds than any other state. Numerous 13 to 15-pounders are caught each year, but larger bass are rare. When giants near 18 pounds are caught, though, often it is from a small mill pond. In a state with thousands of ponds, predicting which one will produce a monster is difficult.

Even relatively unknown waters may yield a behemoth. The lake record for most waters of ten acres or more usually exceeds 14 pounds and many have some bass in the range of 17 pounds or better to brag about. Numerous waters have some reasonable expectation for yielding several dozen largemouth over 10 pounds each. Larger waters, if healthy, have more potential.

Some of the mid-to-small size waters that don't generally receive as much attention (from the press or anglers) produce trophy bass. Some even yield a greater number of giants per overall pounds-per-acre than do others.

A few springs ago, one of the largest bass ever caught in the state was taken from a small "unnamed" panhandle pond. Donald Brunson of Geneva, Florida, caught the monster, and his fish might have had a legitimate shot at the 20-pound, 2-ounce state record had it not been out of the water for several hours before being officially weighed. It was initially weighed on a produce scale at 19-pounds 2-ounces and then again five hours later on certified scales at 18-pounds 8-ounces.

The 56-year old Brunson, a confirmed lunker hunter with a 16-pounder and other big panhandle largemouth to his credit, is after the next world record. He believes it will come from waters 30 miles either side of a line drawn from Lake Juniper to Lake Jackson, in the panhandle. Lakes Victor, Smith, Hurricane and several small mill ponds have all produced monster bass in years past. The typical mill ponds in south Georgia and northwest Florida have plenty of 6-foot water and giant bass.

"I'll normally fish the shallow bedding areas where I can cast to the deeper stretches," Brunson says. "My favorite big bass bait is a black, 7-inch plastic salamander with a modified head. I like to fish it after dark. That's when I've caught most of my really big bass."

On Hurricane Lake near Munson in the panhandle, a 17-pound, 8-ounce bass was taken by another angler a few years ago. To get a feel for the geographic range of the Florida trophies, though, also consider a monster bass that was taken from a small, natural lake in central Florida a few summers ago. Bill Oberry, of Seffner, wrestled the line-class world record to the boat on July 6th, a time when females of significant size are seldom caught.

The giant bass, measuring 30 inches in length and 22 1/2 inches in girth, hit a yellow/green skirted spinnerbait as it fell from a clump of maidencane into eight feet of water. The fish immediately swam away from the grass shoreline toward Oberry's aluminum boat. It never jumped but frequently spun the boat during the battle. The 14-pound monofilament held and his wife netted the fish. It was certified until two days later after it had been frozen. The "official" mark was 17-pounds, 4-ounces.

The clear water lake that 42-year old Oberry is reluctant to name has several deep holes, which is unusual for most waters in the state. He's been fishing the Polk County lake for five years and likes its out-of-the-way location.

Donald Bunson caught this 18-pound, 8-ounce bass from a small panhandle pond. He was tossing a 7-inch long plastic salamander from the shallows to deep water.

On another remote Central Florida lake, Mike Paule caught a 17 1/2-pounder that measured 28 inches in length and 25 inches in girth. Paule caught the huge bass on a black/silver broken-back Rapala tossed along a weed line in 8 feet of water. The bass was allowed to lay on the floor of the boat and was weighed nine hours later on certified scales. It was probably a lake record for Lake Rose, a 40-acre private lake in West Orange County.

The phosphate pits of Polk County are another reason why Central Florida trophy seekers think any world record shot may come from that part of the state. They are always growing huge largemouth. Most are located south of Interstate 4 (between Orlando and Tampa) in the Mulberry/Lakeland area. Each year,several fish over 13 pounds are pulled from the reclaimed waters. Unfortunately, many are private waters, but some do exist that are open to the public.

Phosphate pit angling is often a unique experience for anglers familiar with the state's shallow, natural lakes. Structure fishermen are most often responsible for the super giants that lie in the deeper pit waters that often stretch to 30 or 40 feet. Naturally, the spring spawning urge puts most of the heavyweights in a vulnerable position. Fortunately, the most popular public pits, nine Tenoroc State Reserve lakes, are tightly regulated to protect a trophy fishery.

The State Reserve near Lakeland provides anglers public access to some of the best big bass pit angling available. Opened in late 1983, it has produced numerous 10-pound plus largemouth since, but many monsters swim in the lakes that are open to permit holders. A 16-pound largemouth was electroshocked by Florida Game and Fresh Water Fish Commission biologists from Lake B on the Tenoroc Fish Management Area. The 27 1/2-inch-long female was the second largest bass ever sampled by the state fisheries people. A 14-pound 3-ounce bass also was shocked up in the Reserve's "fly fishing only" lake.

Big Water Giants

Not all big fish come from small Florida waters. The shallow flats of bulrush and maidencane that are so abundant on the 22,700-acre West Lake Tohopekaliga are the home of monster largemouth. Located south of Kissimmee in Osceola County off highway 441 and the Florida Turnpike, it produced a lake record just last year. Toho, as it is commonly known, gave up the 17-pound, 12-ounce largemouth bass in July to John Faircloth of Kissimmee.

The Kissimmee resident was fishing in the late afternoon from the bank. He was casting an 8-inch worm to the opposite shore where the depth was approximately 8 feet. The 28-inch long fish hit a red shad-colored worm in the stained waters of Shingle Creek at the mouth of the lake. The plastic wiggler was "Texas-rigged" with 1/16 ounce slip sinker and 4/0 Tru-Turn hook attached to 14-pound Trilene.

Faircloth knew where the big fish was hiding out, since he had lost it just one week earlier. The giant bass had broken the rod then and escaped. This time the fish wasn't so lucky. The hooked fish again tried to dive into cypress snags. Faircloth fought the monster

The phosphate pits of Polk County are big bass havens. This 16 pounder was electroshocked by the Florida Game and Fresh Water Fish Commission at the popular Tenoroc Reserve.

bass in the late afternoon heat for 20 minutes before landing it.

Naturally, there is speculation that Faircloth's largemouth with an additional year of growth and carrying roe might have had a legitimate shot at the state record: a 20-pound 2-ounce largemouth caught from a private lake near Tampa in 1923.

Lots of big fish have been taken from West Lake Tohopekaliga over the years. Numerous monsters in the 14 and 15-pound class and a 20-fish stringer weighing 148.23 pounds caught by a man and wife back in 1977 have been taken from the lake.

Toho is the sixth largest natural lake in the state, with a maximum depth of only 15 feet. The lake has abundant grass flats in three to seven foot depths. Brown's Point off the southwestern shore has productive bulrush beds that jut out into the lake several hundred

Trophy largemouth in West Lake Tohopekaliga, like John Faircloth's 17-pound, 12-ounce giant, usually fall for big live baits or Texas-rigged worms.

yards. Huge largemouth lie in many of the interior beds, and in the late spring, many are on the outer edges of the rushes. Paradise Island, the west shore, Lanier Point and Friar's Cove in the southeast corner of Toho are productive, as are the grass patches around Whaley's Landing and directly across on the south shore.

Further north, on the St. Johns River, Buddy Wright's first cast late one April evening was pounced on by a feisty five-pound largemouth. He quickly worked that fish to his boat and released it. He worked his Weed Walker spoon back over the same grass several times and was about to move further down the bank when the monster bass struck as the lure neared the boat.

The angler saw the side of the largemouth "flash" in the shallow water when it came out of the stringy vegetation below the boat to

The St. Johns River produces a lot of big fish, such as this 18-pound, 13-ounce monster caught by Buddy Wright. The bass followed a Norman Weed Walker spoon from shallow vegetation.

grab the weedless spoon. The huge largemouth bulled back toward the eel grass as Wright watched the fish bury itself. The skilled angler, who has a 13 and 15-pounder to his credit, knew that he had on an even larger one than the two on his wall.

The giant finally emerged from the shallow grass and Wright grabbed the fish's tail. The roe-laden female was lifted over the gunwale of his 14-foot boat and placed in the cooler, but it wouldn't fit. Wright headed for the scales which revealed that the monster

This 28-inch long largemouth was pulled from a 40-acre lake in Central Florida. It weighed 17 1/2 pounds and struck a minnow plug fished over 8 feet of water beside a weedline.

weighed 18 pounds, 13 ounces. That fish was the largest bass taken in Florida over the past 26 years and the third largest ever.

Big Fish Waters

Numerous other trophy lakes are spread around the state. In north central Florida, the 3 1/2 mile-long Newnan Lake near the outskirts of Gainesville is a prime big fish producer. The cypress trees and shallow, brush-filled coves are the home for many fish over

Harry Woods landed this 15-pound, 2-ounce beauty while fishing for panfish with his cane pole. Sunset Lake is only 10 acres and typical of many small Florida waters with giant bass.

ten pounds. Crankbaits and spinnerbaits account for numerous bass up to 14 pounds here. Lake Kerr, located near the small village of Salt Springs in the Ocala National Forest, is generous to those with the patience and knowledge to attract the lunkers from its crystal clear water. Giant bass in the 2,800 acre lake are shallow in the spring and more vulnerable then.

A little further south and west, near Inverness, Lake Tsala Apopka is a trophy fishery with a lake record of over 15 pounds established in 1989. The 19,000 acre chain of lakes is full of all types of aquatic vegetation. Big Henderson, Little Henderson, Little Spivey, Big Spivey and Lake Davis are the better bass fisheries there. The Kissimmee River gave up a 16 pounder to a Kentucky visitor a couple of years ago.

An armfull of bass over 15 pounds have been taken from Lake Lochloosa and Rodman Reservoir, both near Gainesville, on live shiners around vegetation. Tiny Buffum Lake in southern Polk County produced a 15-pound, 7-ounce largemouth for a Lake Wales

FLORIDA'S TROPHY LIST

Big Bass Water	Top Bait(s)	Top Method(s)
Lake Carr/Jackson	Black Jitterbug and huge worms	Snaked across marsh areas over 2 to 5 foot depths
Crescent Lake	Crankbaits and topwater plugs	Fished next to rush beds in 4 to 6 feet of water
East Lake Toho	Plastic worms	Worked through the rushes in 6 to 8 feet of crystal clear water at night
Lake Kissimmee	Topwater spoons	Fished in the grass and pad beds in 3 to 6 foot depths
Lake Okeechobee	Weedless spoons Native shiners	Snaked across the sawgrass Fished under bobber against grass in 3 to 5 feet of water
Orange Lake	Plastic eels and worms Huge shiners	Flippin' the grass and pads in 4 to 6 feet of water Submarined under floating hyacinths in 8 foot depths
Phosphate Pits (Polk County)	Jig-and-eel	Fished on brushy humps in 8 to 15 feet of water
Sandhill Ponds (in Panhandle)	Spinnerbaits and spoons	Snaked through pad-filled bogs in 4 to 8 feet of stained water
St. Johns River (near Georgetown)	Plastic worms Minnow plugs	Fished off tide-influenced points in 4 to 7 foot depths Fished near cover in spring runs
St. Johns River (near Sanford)	Native shiners	Worked in outer river bends in 4 to 8 foot depths
West Lake Toho	Plastic worms Huge shiners	Flippin' the rushes in 4 to 8 feet of water Fished under corks along the boat trail in 3 to 6 foot depths

angler. Some other central Florida bodies of water with a trophy bass reputation are: Lake Panasoffkee near the town of that name, Lake Harris near Leesburg, the Withlacoochee River backwaters near Dunnellon, and Lake Monroe near Sanford. The Apalachicola River and Dead Lake in the panhandle, and Lakes Tarpon, Crescent, and George as well as the Oklawaha River in north-central Florida provide lots of big bass action. Southward, consider Lake June-In-The-Winter, East Lake Tohopekaliga, Istokpoga and the Conservation area canals.

Look over the Trophy Lake List and study the proven lunker techniques for each water. Those methods have always worked in the past and will again fool the monsters this year, whether used on those waters or on less publicized ones.

You don't even have to have heavy-duty bass gear to catch a lunker in the state, as Harry Woods of Mascotte, Florida found out. He established the NFWFHOF Pole and Line Division (no reel) heaviest largemouth while fishing with a cane pole and live minnows for crappie. The 15-pound 2-ounce bass was caught on February 1 from the 10-acre Sunset Lake west of Clermont. He fought it for 20 minutes releasing the pole twice and following it with his small boat!

A man from Martin County caught a 15 pound largemouth and he didn't even have a pole. He was clearing cattails and debris from a small private canal with a backhoe when the bucket scooped up the monster bass. So the tackle, size of water or your intentions don't really matter, when it comes to landing outsized trophy bass in Florida!

2 / CALIFORNIA DREAMING

World Record Chase Continues

IT USED TO stand for beaches, bikinis and rock bands. That was in the 1960's, when California Dreamin' meant something else. Today, you can add another word, make that two words, to that thought: Trophy Bass.

Over the last several years, California has produced more huge largemouth bass than any other state. Florida, Virginia and Texas are also the standard bearers of giant largemouth, all producing documented catches exceeding 16 pounds. But the far west state produces more such giants.

Fisheries managers in California introduced Florida-strain large-mouth into state waters in the late 60's, and since then, their trophy bass fishery has been unparalleled. In the mid to late 70's, San Diego city lakes began producing huge bass, including the 20 pound, 15 ounce Lake Miramar specimen. The success spread to other state waters, and they, too, began producing numerous bass between 15 and 20 pounds.

With the new state record 21 pound, 3.2 ounce Lake Casitas bass caught in 1980, California had firmly established a reputation for producing monster bass. Add to that the fact that fishermen today have become more conservation-minded and often release big fish, and you have a prospering trophy bass fishery.

Lunker bass hunters continue assaulting lake records in California, but the state record set in 1980, and George Perry's 22-pound 4-ounce world standard bearer, remain unchanged. Anglers there, and those visiting, dream of topping the ultimate largemouth record, while others far away in cooler climates are making strides of their own toward state records of smaller proportions. Trophy fishermen of the far west are more conservation-minded, and a new state mark becomes more realistic. Each year for the past 10, huge largemouth have been coming from their fish factories.

"The conditions from year to year have more to do with the number of big bass caught than anything else," explains Jim Brown, San Diego City Lakes Manager. "Pressure can affect a fishery, though. San Diego waters have pressure that people in the South can't understand."

At Lake Hodges in the spring time, for example, about one person per acre will fish the lake each day, according to Brown. To put that in perspective, that's about 1,000 people on Hodges, or 180,000 anglers on Toledo Bend Reservoir, or 450,000 fishermen on Lake Okeechobee. That has to be considered intense pressure. Hodges, despite tremendous pressure, is undoubtedly one of the best trophy bass lakes in the country.

Why? The reason is simple, according to Brown. The lake level has been stable for a number of years, allowing cattails to grow around its perimeter. The fish find refuge in that vegetation which runs out to 8 or 9 feet of water. The cover is excellent.

"In 1987, the water level was lower than in past years and the bass were pretty much flushed out of the cover," says Brown. "With the total cover available to them decreased, the big bass were a lot more vulnerable."

"From my standpoint of managing a recreation program, Hodges is the ideal lake," opts Brown. "It produces two pounders that the average angler is capable of catching, and produces good numbers of 6 and 7 pounders which the average fishermen have a good shot at and the good fishermen can tap out. It also produces the real trophies that the average fisherman using bait can catch and a very skilled angler may get a shot at. It has something for everybody!"

The Hodges Score Sheet

Lake Hodges is the best of California's "non-trout" lakes. In the late-80's, the lake yielded 124 over nine pounds, and most of those,

Lake Hodges produced both of these lunkers. Gene Dupras established lake records with a 17-pound, 7-ounce giant (L) and later, with a 20-pound, 4-ounce monster (R).

along with two in the 14-pound class, were spring catches from the expansive shallows that contribute to the lake's high bass growth rate. After the second year, the females average about a pound of growth each year. There is adequate surface acreage on Hodges with very little depth, another reason for high productivity.

On Lake Hodges in the mid-80's, the fourth largest bass ever caught in the world (numbers two and three were also taken in California) fell victim to a live, 3 1/2-inch long crayfish. Gene Dupras of Lakeside caught the 20-pound 4-ounce largemouth on his first cast to some short stick-ups and rocks. The trophy bass specialist also had an earlier lake record with a 17-pound 7-ounce fish. Dupras tosses a nose-hooked crayfish on 16-pound test line into water depths ranging from 15 to 25 feet and "walks" it back to the boat. With the two mounted bass totaling almost 38 pounds, Dupras has some great "company."

Lake Hodges, which yielded eight bass over 15 pounds one year in the mid-80's, was certainly California's big bass "star." The lake also yielded largemouth of 17-pounds 11-ounces, 17-pounds 4-ounces, and 16-pounds 1-ounce. The latter came during a major tournament and is reputed to be the largest ever during competition.

31

Other Spots To Dream About

Lake Castaic, near Los Angeles, produced a 16 pound, 14 ounce largemouth on a worm and jig and several others over 15 pounds in the mid-60's. Then, a true trophy chaser, Dan Kadota of San Pedro, California, came along. The offshore charter boat captain spends his off days in the freshwater lakes of southern California and has personally caught 27 largemouth in just three years with his big bass strategy. That's impressive enough, but consider that one of the largemouth weighed 19.04 pounds and another 18.75 pounds. Throw in a pair of 14 pounders caught on the same day, and you should have an appreciation of his methods and Lake Castaic.

Kadota is a dedicated lunker bass hunter who studies the lake bottom to determine subtle changes in topography. He'll spends hours on the water with his electronics interpreting the information. He'll analyze the data to define bass access routes and then carefully figure how to mark the spots and position the boat for the best opportunity at a trophy-size bass.

His expertise with sonar has been established in salt water, and he utilizes it to the fullest on Lake Castaic. Wind and current direction, as well as time of day, influence his boat positioning. Anchoring is done to keep the rope away from the bass routes. The captain even uses two anchors, one fore and one aft, at times, and repositions his boat similarly to having a pulley system, by pulling closer to one anchor while letting out rope to the other.

Live bait such as waterdogs, crayfish or shad, are Kadota's normal offering to the oversized bass, and they often work. He admittedly fishes two or three days with very little success for every one successful trophy day. That's part of the science of big bass angling, according to the man who, with a partner, caught a 10-bass limit that weighed almost 95 pounds.

California's "trout lakes," those which offer the high protein forage on a regular basis, usually produce some extremely heavy largemouth. Trout have a lot of fat tissue and the bass that feed on them voraciously in the late fall develop thick layers of fat. The state normally stocks 30 to 50 pounds of trout per acre in October and November. Using trout as bait is illegal, so live shiners and crayfish are responsible for many of the true giants caught.

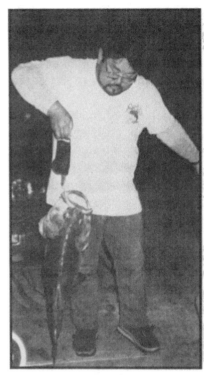 

Lunker hunter, Dan Kadota, has his hands full with this 19-pound, 1 ounce Lake Castaic monster. The lake is not a San Diego dream water; it's nearer Los Angeles.

Lake Wohlford gave up 1986's biggest California bass, a 19-pound, 3-ounce specimen. The fish, caught by Jerry Beasley on a golden shiner, is the largest taken from the 146-acre lake. At least two fish over 17 pounds have been brought to the scales. Another Escondido City reservoir with a trout-based food chain, Lake Dixon, has produced 16 pound bass. The official lake record on Lake Jennings of 16-pounds 5-ounces has been set twice in the 80's. In the past few years, Lake Vail produced over 100 nine-pound plus bass, including a 17-pound, 12-ounce giant.

More 18-Pound Bets

Lake Miramar, which received a lot of attention when it produced Dave Zimmerlee's 20-pound, 15-ounce bass, succumbed to heavy fishing pressure in the late 1970's, but it's back. It gave up a 17-pound 4-ounce trophy in the mid-eighties, and the notorious largemouth of 1988. That fish initially weighed 21 pounds, 10 ounces before a taxidermist found the discarded diver's weight in its stomach. Even at 19 pounds plus, that largemouth was one of the largest ever caught on an artificial lure.

Lake Poway yielded the largest bass in the entire country one year, a 17 pound, 8 ounce giant to a 15 year old boy fishing from shore in Halfmoon Bay. The fish came from 8 feet of water in the late afternoon. The boy, Mike Lanza, caught three other bass weighing 11-pounds, 12-ounces; 12-pounds, 12-ounces; and 13-pounds, 6-ounces that spring. A 16-pound, 8-ounce behemoth and other trophies have been taken since, and the lunkers are still there, fattening up naturally on trout.

Morena Reservoir, a 1600 acre lake at a 3100 foot elevation, seemed to come alive recently with the production of king-size largemouth. A lake record of 19-pounds, 3-ounces was caught by Arden Hanline on a 3-inch Rapala in February of 1987. That fish taken from 49-degree water, bested a 17 pound, 7 ounce mark set the year before. Arden's trophy was landed on 8-pound Trilene line from the east shoreline near Goat Island.

Largemouth weighing almost 18 pounds have been taken recently from Lake Casitas in Ventura County near the city of Ventura. The biggest was caught on a plastic worm fished from shore. Four or five largemouth between 14 and 16 pounds are normally caught from the lake which produced the second largest bass ever: a 21-pound, 3 1/4-ounce Florida-strain in 1980.

The same lake yielded the state's heaviest five-bass stringer in the mid-80's that weighed 64 pounds, 15 ounces. The bass, which included "anchor" fish weighing 16 pounds, 5 ounces and 14 pounds, 10 ounces, were taken on live crayfish and 8 pound test line. Few of today's conservation-minded anglers are still going after that mark.

Lake Isabella, 160 miles north of Los Angeles near Bakersfield, has yielded several giant largemouth in the past few years including a double limit of bass to brothers Steve and Jerry Beasley. The Beasleys' 10 largemouth weighed 107-pounds 7-ounces and came on nose-hooked crayfish from 55-foot depths.

This Lake Poway trophy weighing 17-pounds, 8-ounces, was taken by a 15-year old angler. He was fishing from shore and casting to 8 feet of water in the late afternoon.

The waters have structure such as buildings, a 3-mile long water flume and even an airport in its depths, and giant bass are easy to lose on light line. Isabella can be tough to fish too in the spring when the monsters are more vulnerable. The remote area 40 miles away from the nearest city, Bakersfield, is extremely windy. Despite less than ideal conditions, Isabella bass chasers have captured some half dozen giant largemouth over 18 pounds in just the past three years. The leader of the pack was an 18-pound, 14-ounce monster caught on a live crayfish.

Isabella contains 11,200 surface acres and 38 miles of shoreline for the bass to explore in search of food. The upper elevations of the two Kern River forks offer trout waters, the headwaters of the north fork offering more white water. The southern arm of the reservoir is a shallow, lengthy bass factory with more typical bass habitat.

Lower Otay yielded several bass over 15 pounds including an "unofficial" lake record weighing 19 pounds. San Diego's San Vicente Reservoir has produced 15 pound largemouth, and 60 to 70 bass over nine pounds are normally taken from the 900-acre trout-enriched lake each year.

The trophy bass hunting in California's waters hasn't stopped and neither have the impressive results. Estimates of largemouth over 14 pounds taken each year range from 30 to over 40. Access control and weight certification on many waters, including most of

Lake Miramar gave up the 19 pounder (L) which was not a lake record, and Lake Isabella yielded the 16-pound, 10-ounce trophy (R). Both waters are reputed to have larger fish swimming around.

the San Diego area lakes allow for fairly accurate records. Poor census capabilities do exist, however, on lakes Wohlford, Vail, Dixon, Henshaw, Poway, and Morena.

California has been a big bass producer for years, and it will remain that way for a long time. Since the introduction of Florida-strain largemouth in the late 1960s, that state's trophy bass fishery has been unparalleled.

36

3 TEXAS CRUDE

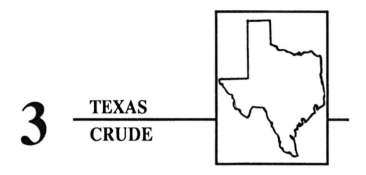

The New Player In Trophy Bass Action

THE LUNKER LARGEMOUTH explosion continues in the Lone-Star state. The future appears promising for ten-pound plus bass opportunities and even a new Texas record bass. Several potential hot spots stand out as consistent producers of trophy fish; still others yield an occasional near-record largemouth. With literally hundreds of good bass fishing lakes in Texas (at least 200 reservoirs are over 5,000 acres) picking the best bets for lunker bass is not easy.

The waters in Texas that have a state record potential and/or produce several bass over ten pounds each year are many. Several of the top waters have restrictions to maintain the quality fishery. A visiting angler should check out special regulations, such as slot limits, minimum length limits, etc., prior to his fishing trip.

An impoundment stocked with Florida bass in the early 1980's seems to have a grasp on the record book currently. Lake Fork Reservoir has special regulations in place and the potential to be at the top of the state's trophy class waters for years. The 27,000-acre reservoir 75 miles east of Dallas produced the current Texas state record largemouth. Caught by guide Mark Stevenson in November of 1986, it weighed 17-pounds, 10.72-ounces. The 27.4 inch long bass hit a jig and worm trailer as it was crawled along a 15 foot ridge bordering a 24-foot deep ditch.

That mark may not be in effect long, since the same cover-laden lake is producing huge bass at a hot clip. A 17-pound, 4-ounce largemouth, the second largest Texas bass to date, was also taken from Fork in February of 1988. The fish was fooled by a black jig and pork trailer fished in submerged brush at about 15 feet. Another bass weighing approximately 17 1/2 pounds washed up on North Fork Marina's boat ramp during the same week. Another dead floater weighing 19.62 pounds was found that spring. Cause of deaths were unknown.

Plenty of other live giants have been caught there in the past few years, including a 16-pound, 9-ounce largemouth. In fact, a majority of the top 20 largemouth on Texas' latest "Top 50 Bass List" have come from the lake. That's quite a record for any one lake in a state that has hundreds of waters with Florida bass transplants. Many Texans are predicting that the next world record bass will come from Lake Fork, and they might be right.

A 16-pound, 14 1/2-ounce largemouth caught from Lake Pinkston in Shelby County is currently the third largest Texas bass. Earl Crawford caught the 27 5/8 inch long fish in 15 feet of water on a crawfish-colored crankbait. The lakeside resident was using 17-pound test Berkley Trilene. Ironically, he was born in a house on the lake bed (now inundated by water) not far from his big catch.

The pure Florida-strain monster is indicative of fisheries genetics initiated on largemouth bass in the early 70's by the Parks and Wildlife Department. The Florida-strain bass were stocked in the spring creek-fed Pinkston in 1976, and the 560-acre lake has produced numerous lunkers in the past two years. The lake record was determined to be one of the initial transplants. Pinkston has also yielded a 14-pounder making those little waters hot.

Just last year, Mill Creek produced a 16-pound, 12-ounce monster, and a shad-colored crankbait fooled a 16 pounder in Gibbons Creek. A 16-pound Possum Kingdom Reservoir bass caught in late 1989 is the largest to be taken to date in the western half of the state. Both waters could easily yield a new state record, as could the 1981 record breaker water, Echo Lake. Although it is just 175 acres, it produced two former state records, both to John Alexander, Jr.

Catching big bass from the deep takes patience, hard work and a basic knowledge of their behavior. Alexander, of Richardson, is the only two-time largemouth bass state record holder in Texas history and his lunker techniques exemplify the above requirements.

Lake Fork has produced many of the state's monster largemouth in the last year or two, including this 17-pound, 11-ounce trophy. It was caught by guide Mark Stevenson on a jig-and-worm combo.

He caught several trophy bass from the seemingly flat and shallow lake near Athens, Texas. The average depth of the spring-fed lake, which has two creeks at its headwaters, is 16 feet. Plenty of submerged structure and drop-offs, coontail moss and flooded trees in two coves provide excellent habitat for the bass and their forage.

Despite the near shore cover, Alexander reasoned that the really big bass would be found in the deeper holes during the cool weather months. In 1980, Alexander spent 287 hours after deep water bass. He caught only seven fish during the period, but all exceeded five pounds - the largest 12 pounds, 10 ounces. He inched black jigs with split-tail eel trailers over the many brush piles strewn

Trophy hunter John Alexander caught two state records in the early 1980's from tiny Echo Lake. Other small waters around the state have the Florida bass that made this lake famous.

about. The depth averaged 25 feet at the mouth of the two coves.

He wanted the Texas record and his persistence paid off. From the same general area in a two month period the following year, he caught the state records: a 15 1/2 pounder and a 14 pound, 3 1/2 ounce bass. In addition he caught two over 13 pounds, two over 12 pounds and four over 11 pounds.

Other Trophy Spots

Stocked initially in 1974 with 74,000 Florida bass, Houston County Lake is usually rated near the top in the state in hours-per-trophy bass. A high average weight for largemouth creel results assure that this 1,485-acre water will continue to be among the very

The fish that started in all, the 13-pound, 8-ounce Texas record that stood for 37 years. Today, it's not even on the state's Top 50 Bass List.

best in ten pound or better fish. A 15-pound 3-ounce monster is the lake's largest to date. Big bass production there remains high.

Houston County Lake was formed by damming Little Elkhart Creek, the main feeder, and other tiny watersheds. Depth at the dam is about 40 feet and while the water there is open, several submerged islands and creek channels are present. The reservoir, located midway between Houston and Dallas twenty minutes east of Interstate 45, is maintained at a constant level.

Lake Jacksonville produced two trophies recently, a 27 1/2-inch long, 15-pound 2-ounce lunker and a 14-pound 6 3/4-ounce largemouth. Florida bass were introduced each year from 1975 on into Jacksonville, resulting in a stable fishery that is now producing lunkers. One-half million Florida-strain bass have been stocked into the 1,350-acre lake over the years.

Lake Welch is one of the hottest producers of lunker bass in Texas. The 1,400-acre power plant lake received its stipend of Florida bass beginning in 1975 and produced a 15-pound 4-ounce monster. Nearby Lake Monticello, stocked in 1973 with Florida bass, is also still one of the premier trophy lakes in Texas. The 2,000-

Florida bass, like this 16-pound, 9-ounce trophy that Guy Witherspoon caught in Lake Fork, are responsible for the big bass explosion in Texas waters. Look for the Lone Star state to produce a 20 pounder in the near term.

acre waters have yielded at least three bass over 14 pounds, including a short-lived state record.

The longest running big bass show in the state, Lake Murvaul, has a superior strain of northern bass that grow to oversize proportions. The 3,800-acre lake is the best for northern-strain trophy bass (no Florida bass trophies yet) and usually sits at the top in the annual Texas Parks & Wildlife survey's hours-per-trophy-bass ranking.

Most of these trophy waters are stocked with the Florida bass strain which has caused more than a stir among state bass record chasers. Well over a hundred Texas lakes have been stocked with the strain by the Texas Parks and Wildlife (TP&W) Department, but not all introductions have been successful.

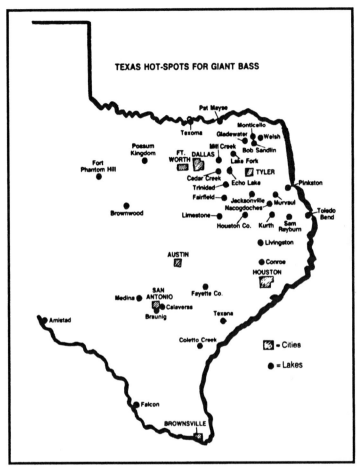

FIGURE 1 - *There are plenty of waters around Texas that have the potential of producing trophy bass. These are just a few of the "hawg hole" in the state.*

The explosion of the Florida bass and the hybrid 'superbass' (cross between the northern and the Florida-strain largemouths) have catapulted many waters into the limelight. Other lakes are perennial big bass (northern strain) producers and are currently holding their own against the hot new lakes with Florida bass and/or heated (power plant) waters.

The results of the TP&W efforts have shown that new impoundments have the greatest chances of maximum Florida bass survival, and in general, the quickest resulting trophy bass fishery. This is greatly enhanced if the lake is given a head start on the fishing pressure, that is, having it initially closed to fishing for 2 or 3 years and then opened 'gradually' to preclude an 'opening day' slaughter (which has occurred in the past on more than one Texas lake).

Potential Lunker Holes

Several large waters with the potential to yield a trophy exist. In the past 10 years, well over 2 million Florida bass have been stocked in Lake Amistad, a 65,000-acre Rio Grande River impoundment. A jig and pig recently produced a 15.58 pound largemouth that is the largest every caught in the western half of Texas.

Initial stocking of Florida bass began in 1975 and Lake Falcon is beginning to produce trophy fish. Several five to seven pounders makes a bright future possible for the 99,000-acre Rio Grande border lake. Always a producer of many six-pound-plus bass, Lake Livingston has an established Florida bass population in the upper end (surveys have shown 30 percent Florida strain in many coves). Largemouth to 10 pounds are fairly common in the spring on the 90,000-acre lake.

Lake Athens, a 1,500 acre water district lake, has produced numerous big bass, including a 27 3/4 inch bass that weighed a few ounces shy of 14 pounds. Nacogdoches Lake, impounded in 1977, was severely hurt by the "opening day" effect when 12,000 pounds of Florida bass were taken in a few days. Special restrictions have allowed the 2,210-acre fishery to come back, and a few trophies, such as a 14 pounder taken in 1986, are being taken.

Small ponds and lakes around the state do provide excellent opportunities for many anglers to catch lunker size largemouth. Production of trophy bass is optimum for waters above two surface acres in size, and many of the small private lakes have better fishery management than the super small ponds. Often, the best smaller waters are far from the large impoundments, such as several great ones in southwest Texas (near Brownsville, Laredo, and Carrizo Springs).

4 SOUTHERN BELLES

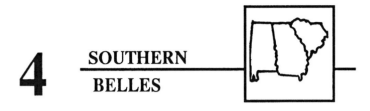

Pretty "Hawgs" Around The South

IT WAS COLD outside. Jim Smith knew that as he lay in bed thinking about where to go fishing. He had already charged his electric motor, and after all, his "Pepsi Cola Fishing Calendar" had said that March day would be the best of the month. It wasn't until his second cup of coffee that he decided on Mims Mill Pond, a small pay-to-fish pond south of Moultrie, Georgia.

He knew every tree stump in the tannic-stained waters. The 46-year old draftsman had fished there since he was ten years old and, in fact, caught his first bass there. The pond, like so many mill ponds in north Florida and south Georgia, is primarily fished by locals who pay a small fee. On this day, as Smith launched his 10-foot boat at the crack of dawn, he found the pond all to himself.

Action came fast. His third cast with a black Bang-O-Lure to a stump surrounded by weeds attracted a 3-pound largemouth. Twenty feet down the bank, he caught a 7 pounder and then, just past another stump, two more small ones that he released. He twitched the minnow across the fork of a submerged tree and the fish hit. It churned at the surface and came out of the water on the first jump.

Smith proceeded to play the fish carefully as it jumped another 3 times, swam under the boat and finally became exhausted towing the boat around the pond. He grabbed the bass by its lower jaw and threw it into the boat. That was his last cast that day. Just one hour after arriving at the pond he headed for the local postmaster's scales where he weighed his 20-pound, 1-ounce largemouth. Smith has caught several bass between 10 and 12 pounds, but nothing close to that 29 1/4-inch long specimen. The girth of Smith's new line-class world record set on March 25, 1989 was 26 1/4 inches.

The monster bass was obviously the largest ever taken from Mims Mill Pond, which had, according to owner Essie Mims, yielded bass between 14 and 18 pounds over the years. Locals that fish many of the other numerous mill ponds in that part of the Georgia can relate catches of 16 to 19 pounds. Each year, a giant bass or two is taken from the small ponds, but the word is usually slow to spread. Allatoona Lake with a recent 16-pound, 8-ounce bass is a potential trophy spot. It takes something that large to garner anyone's attention when the state record is also the world record.

A huge largemouth reported to be 36 3/4 inches long and 35 inches around its girth made Georgia headlines in the mid-80's. The fish, supposedly weighing 22-pounds, 3 1/4-ounces, was caught from a farm pond. As often happens in trying to confirm reports of new world records, or near-world records, little documented evidence of this catch existed. The "angler" supposedly ate the bass, and pictures couldn't be located. Reports of larger fish occur in other states every few years, but none have ever been confirmed. Seems like most all of the largemouth between 22 and 30 pounds caught make excellent table fare and do not photograph well!

Alabama Tide

There are no complaints from Alabama anglers about the growth of Florida bass in their waters either. The last three and probably four state records have been the Florida strain. A 16-pound, 8-ounce largemouth is the current leader in the state's push toward world recognition as a trophy producer. But the fact that the Florida bass now exist in every reservoir in Alabama bodes eventual obsolescence for the record set only in September, 1987.

The state jumped into stocking the Florida strain ahead of many. Since 1975, Alabama has introduced the species into all state-stocked waters, including both private ponds and huge impoundments. Most of their stockings occurred in 1980 and 1981, and their fishery biologists expect those fish and their first offspring (intergrades) to take about eight years before appearing as trophy size

Bass like this 15-pound, 8-ounce giant can be found around the South.

bass. After watching California and Texas successes, they are now convinced that their fishery has great potential.

The reason why a nine-pound largemouth is not unusual coming out of Lake Eufaula or West Point Lake is because those fish are intergrades. The bass in west Alabama are mostly northern strain, and a nine pounder there is very rare. The waters are at the exact same latitude, but the fish are different.

It doesn't take a big reservoir to produce fish like this 17-pound, 9-ounce largemouth. Numerous tiny lakes are responsible for similar catches around the South.

Alabama's state record bass was recently taken from the private Mountain View Lake in Shelby County. It weighed 16 1/2 pounds and was taken in November by T. M. Burgin. He was using a 6-inch motor oil-colored worm fished in 15 feet of water. Interestingly, the 29 1/2 inch long bass was a northern strain largemouth that had no egg formations. Had the fish been caught in February, it could have weighed 20 pounds, according to a state fisheries biologist.

Burgin's fish eclipsed the previous Alabama largemouth record of 15-pounds, 9-ounces, set just two months earlier. That fish and previous record holders from Washington County Lake were Florida bass.

South Carolina's largemouth bass fishing is well-established, and quite a few trophies are caught each year. The state record stands at 16-pounds, 2-ounces. It was taken many years ago from Lake Marion. That lake and Lake Moultrie in Santee Cooper County are still top spots for big bass. South Carolina is due for a new record largemouth, so the old one's time may be about up.

5 WORLDLY LUNKERS

State Record Possibilities Exist

EVERY ANGLER DREAMS of catching that state or world record fish, but few really go after one. In fact, putting your name in the record book may be relatively easy. Two friends and I once focused on line-class world records in three categories and succeeded on our first trip out. I won't kid you, the easy records to set usually don't last long, but for a few months or years, you can have a place in angling history.

"There's one new world record set almost each day of the year," points out Bob Kutz, Founder of the National Freshwater Fishing Hall of Fame. "And, for every established record, another catch just as large or larger is voided during documentation to authenticate the record. Other certain records are eaten."

Many people feel that most fish records, particularly those for largemouth bass, have reached their ultimate size limits, but that's far from the truth, according to Kutz. Several state marks are set each year. A lot of people too, pass up the opportunity to become a record holder. Many still are unaware that record systems exist with the Hayward, Wisconsin-based Hall and with the International Game Fish Association (IGFA), which also qualifies salt water fish species from their headquarters in Fort Lauderdale, Florida. (See Appendix for addresses)

Other anglers may be afraid that publicity of their "secret" lunker spot will get out. Still others may feel that the documentation requirements involve too much detail and book work. Assuming that an interested angler can overcome his possible objections to the publicity and documentation realities, plenty of opportunities exist to establish a new state largemouth record tomorrow.

Not all giants caught this year will be over 16 or 17 pounds. Other northern waters that may produce smaller-dimension state record (or near) largemouth this year are New York's Buckhorn Lake and Rhode Island's Wordens Pond. Southern big bass waters also include Lakes Mallard and Millwood in Arkansas and Mississippi's Tippah County Lake, Maynor Creek and Lake Bill Waller.

Virginia has been among the stars in huge largemouth bass production over the past several years. Sixteen-pounders in both 1984 and 1985 set state records. Nothing came along in 1986 to eclipse their state mark of 16-pounds 4-ounces. That record largemouth was taken on a white spinnerbait around noon and died shortly afterwards. The fish was weighed five hours later at a local weigh station and pushed the scales to 16 pounds, 10 1/2 ounces. The difference in the certified weight was due to the state record certifying committee rule that a fish weight must be witnessed by a commission representative. The "official" weighing was a day later.

Lake Conners, a Commission-owned lake in Halifax County, is known as the premier water in the state for producing hefty bass. Its huge bass are thought to be Florida-strain introductions from several years ago. Most of the lakes receiving the stockings froze the winter following the introduction, and Lake Conners is apparently the only lake in which the strain survived. It produced the state record largemouth, the fourth largest bass on record, a 14-pound, 15-ounce fish and a 14-pound, 12-ounce largemouth.

A 15-pound, 6-ounce largemouth was taken from Buggs Island Reservoir. The 30-inch long bass was one of the largest ever taken in the state, as was a 16-pound largemouth taken from a private pond in Halifax County. Virginia's Lake Anna offers more opportunities for big fish, and there are others.

Kentucky's Woods Creek Lake and Lake Malone are trophy producers. The current state record was set in 1984 by a 13-pound, 10.25-ounce largemouth from Woods Creek. A black spinnerbait with 4-inch split-tail pork eel fished around a boulder in 5 feet of water in pre-dawn darkness enticed the trophy.

Virginia produces some giant bass, like this 16-pound, 4-ounce largemouth. The Lake Conners' fish fell for a white spinnerbait at high noon.

Mid-West Trophies

In Oklahoma, several state records were set in the 80's. A 12-pound, 1.6-ounce largemouth caught in 1983 from Lake Lawtonka broke a record established in 1941. The 11-year old intergrade (Florida/northern bass cross) hit a jig-and-pork frog beside an old tree. Lake Humphreys produced another first generation intergrade in 1987 that weighed 5 ounces more. That fish hit a black jig-and-eel fished in six feet of water. Another fish of that same weight was caught the following spring from a private lake in Stephens County. That fish, like an 11 1/2 pounder taken by the same angler the day before, hit a white spinnerbait.

51

This 12-pound, 6-ounce largemouth from a private lake in Oklahoma was a record holder for a short time. The fish was a 12-year old native northern bass.

In 1989, Lake Ozzie Cobb yielded a 12-pound, 10-ounce bass, and two weeks later, Bill Gilbert of Norman, fishing a plastic lizard, broke the record with a 12-pound, 13-ounce lunker from Lake Fuqua. Both lakes have Florida bass introductions, as do Wayne Wallace, Waurika, Konawa, Dripping Springs, Sardis, Murray and other potential trophy producers. I expect more records to follow.

In Minnesota, the state mark was set in 1986. Tim Kirsch pulled an 8-pound 9 1/2-ounce bass from Fountain Lake in the southern part of the state. The Albert Lea resident was trolling an injured-minnow type plug at 6:45 a.m. when the 24 3/4-long fish struck. He was after huge bass specifically and had invested hundreds of hours on the tiny lake in search of the bass he caught.

Nearby South Dakota also set a largemouth bass mark that same year. Irene Buxcel of Belvidere broke the state's 29-year old largemouth record in 1986. She caught the 8-pound 14-ounce fish

Oklahoma recently has been producing more trophy bass, like this 12-pound-plus Lake Lawtonka largemouth, on a fairly regular basis.

from a Jackson County stock pond on a metal-lipped plastic worm. She fought the fish for 20 minutes before pulling it to shore. In Iowa, a state record was recorded in 1984. The 10-pound, 12-ounce largemouth was taken from Lake Fisher on a crankbait.

One of the largest authenticated largemouth ever from Missouri waters fell victim to an Illinois angler. The 13-pound 9-ounce largemouth was only five ounces under the 25-year-old state record. Jay Koren of Joliet, Illinois brought the Truman Reservoir fish to the scales in a regional "Classic" tournament. It was an unusually burly fish, according to regional fisheries biologists for the Conservation Department, who examined the largemouth. The bass age was determined to be at least a dozen years old, which would predate the impoundment where it was caught.

Far West And Beyond

What looked to be a new largemouth bass mark breaking the existing 29-year-old Arizona hook and line record never made it to the record books. The 15-pound largemouth, the largest in the state's history, was illegally taken from Canyon Lake a few years ago.

A Gilbert resident was charged with taking fish with an explosive substance and possessing illegally-taken fish. His state fish record application form was received by the Game and Fish Department on March 15, but certification was initially delayed on technicalities. Then after pictures of the man and his 15-pounder were published in newspapers' outdoor pages, several complaints were received from people who said they knew of someone throwing explosives into Canyon Lake early on the previous Sunday morning.

Scale samples taken from the big bass showed it to be about 8 years old. This supports earlier scale analysis information that shows a very high growth rate for Canyon Lake bass. More 15 pounders, or larger, are probably there, according to the Game and Fish Department. For now though, the 14-pound, 2-ounce specimen taken on hook and line from Lake Roosevelt in 1956 still stands.

A young Apache Indian on the San Carlos Indian Reservation apparently caught, weighed, and then ate a 15-pound plus largemouth. It was taken from a 1 1/2-mile-long Arizona impoundment called Talkalai Lake. The 9-year-old lake was stocked with several large brood Florida bass from a Texas hatchery a few years ago. The nearby San Carlos Lake was also stocked with Floridas and probably gives up more big bass than any other in Arizona.

Even as far away as South Africa, a largemouth record was set in 1987 by a 10-pound, 1-ounce specimen. The fish was caught from Northern Natal's Goedertrouw Dam. A worm fished in 16 feet of water on 12-pound test line was responsible for the strike. Florida bass were first imported into South Africa in 1979, and Goedertrouw received its first stipend in 1981.

A Missouri Conservation Department biologist examines a 13-pound, 9-ounce trophy taken from Truman Reservoir. That lake is one of the best for lunker bass in the "Show Me" state.

Record Assault

The mark that most avid anglers are after is the largemouth bass. The 57-year old, all-tackle record, caught by George Perry in Montgomery Lake, Georgia, is 22-pounds, 4-ounces. Few thought that record would ever be broken until a California bass weighing 21-pounds, 3-ounces was taken in 1980. More recently, in 1989, a 20-pounds, 1-ounce Georgia bass was caught. The Florida state record bass of 20-pounds, 2-ounces was taken in 1923 but was not certified.

The largemouth is certainly the glamour fish in this country and that all-tackle world record is what the masses are shooting at. It could be worth a million dollars in promotion fees and endorsements to the right person. State marks, however, are more reasonable goals for trophy seekers.

Once you have caught a potential world or state record, the documentation process begins. In general, the fish must be weighed on trade-certified scales and witnessed. Clear photographs of the fish, preferably alongside a yardstick, must be taken, and line samples must be sent to the record keeping agency. Affidavits from a fishery biologist, and if possible, from witnesses to the weighing and catch, in addition to one from the angler, are usually required.

For complete details on the procedure to obtain a world record, it's advisable to contact the two world record keeping organizations. Other record-keeping organizations include most of the state fish and game departments. Contact their information officer for details on the state record program and requirements.

The fame and notoriety can be tremendous for some record catches. Recognition is based on commercial significance and/or potential. A largemouth bass all-tackle record would be the ultimate in terms of reward, monetary and recognition. Near record fish and state record marks would normally command less.

Rewards are posted by various tackle companies for record fish caught on their line, lure or rod, and a few organizations and magazines offer large cash prizes for record catches by members or subscribers. Product for life is a popular offer from many manufacturers. Their ads and informational slips/brochures that come with each product usually specify what the reward would consist of.

The most popular world record reward program of all is Berkley's, initiated in June of 1983. For several years, they had a standing cash bonus reward of $1,000 for IGFA line class world records of any recognized sport fish specie caught on Trilene line. The program was restructured for 1990, but over the first four years, about $1,000,000 was paid out on approximately 2,400 records. Several anglers had multiple records, some as many as eight!

6 DISAPPEARING TROPHIES

Are Big Bass In Trouble?

THE SPRING SPAWNING period can be hazardous to trophy bass, since they are shallow and more vulnerable then than at any other time of the year. Some experts believe that 25 percent of the bass over eight pounds are caught every year in just one or two prime bedding months.

That's critical, because an eight pounder is a seven-year replacement resource. For example, when an eight pound largemouth is removed from a body of water, it will normally take a one pound female (males seldom, if ever, reach that weight) about eight years to reach eight pounds. Correspondingly, eight one pounders taken from a body of water would be naturally replaced in 18 months or so by eight fingerlings. Obviously, removing eight pounds of bass from a water is less harmful to the quality of that water if it is in the form of eight smaller, one pounders.

Unfortunately, the word has been slow to spread, and many fish and game agencies have yet to take up the cause. A handful of fishery commissions, Texas and California being the most noteworthy, have focused major effort on the trophy largemouth fishery. It is sad that others, some even with a head start on giant bass, have not.

The trophy bass appears to be in trouble in some areas of the country. Due to pollution problems and angling pressure, many fisheries are on the decline, and unfortunately, the lunker resource appears to be the first affected. Even states with a resurgence of trophy largemouth due partly to introduction of the Florida bass strain, measures need to be taken to protect that new-found legacy. The stocking of the Florida bass will create a new trophy fishery and more giants will be available for a while. The longevity of a trophy fishery, though, seems to depend heavily upon regulation.

Trophy females are most vulnerable while on their beds and that is when the exploitation is most severe. Many are "harvested," as the fishery biologists say, and while the taking of the spawning large-mouth is of concern to many, the Florida G&FWF Commission claims that it is not a legitimate concern.

Large females are generally eight years old and have spawned numerous times and contributed to the gene pool, they say. In addition, few Florida bass survive past ten years of age and may die before being harvested. Furthermore, they point out that egg quality declines after the fish pass their "prime reproductive" years.

It takes at least 10 years for a female bass to reach 12 pounds in Florida. Males seldom exceed four pounds, but any regulation with regard to a trophy fishery must consider the time requirement for bass to reach maximum weights. It is not always considered.

The mortality rate must also be considered and that may vary greatly from lake to lake. The relationship between fishing and natural mortality is not clear, but biologists feel that they probably compensatore each other. In a lake with known fishing pressure, natural mortality can be calculated, and, given the growth rate of its bass, effective regulations can be employed. That's the ideal anyway.

In California, where trophy bass created a stir since introduction in the early 60's, lunker vulnerability and mortality trends closely parallel the water conditions, according to California Fish and Game biologist, Larry Bottroff. Low water conditions and resulting poor recruitment produce lower harvests. When water levels increase, then largemouth catches also rise. Trophy bass harvest is inversely proportional; they are more vulnerable during low water years and catch rates are typically up. During years of high water levels, trophy bass are less prone to being caught.

Regulating The Fishery

Varying regulations have been around for years, and while some state fisheries agencies have been very progressive in their experi-

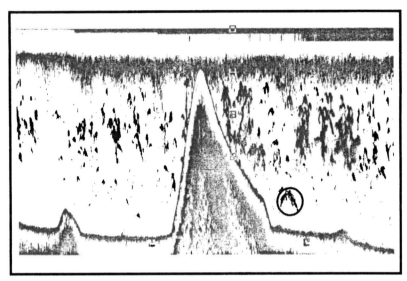

FIGURE 2 - Catching trophies is becoming increasingly more difficult each year. If our generation doesn't "respect and return" big bass, our children will be looking at primarily small fish on their chart recorders.

mentation and trial programs, others have not. Obviously, California, Texas, Missouri and Alabama are among the leaders in developing effective trophy fishery management programs. Sure, there have been failures along with the successes, but for the most part, their insight and foresight has moved many typically conservative state bureaucrats towards progressive management policies.

Although fishing pressure in Southern California doesn't appear to influence a trophy bass fishery as much as water fluctuations, the numbers of angler days are regulated. Angling pressure can affect an increase in harvest of the bass population on the whole, they feel. Thanks to the regulations, the far west trophy largemouth fishery is not in any apparent danger of extinction.

"The harvest rates on catchable bass over 10 inches vary between 25 and 35 percent annually," Bottroff says. "Our reservoirs are not open everyday, and they are usually only open six to eight months each season. That tends to allow a lower harvest rate."

A survey of state regulations in the southeast in 1987 found that every state, except Louisiana, had some special bag, length or slot limit restriction. Oklahoma and Virginia had the most widespread special regulations in effect. Most, happily, have found that slot limit regulations tend to attract more sports anglers and discourage consumptive anglers. Success rates usually improve with the different angler component, according to some state agencies biologists.

Although most state agencies utilize special minimum length limits on some waters, a majority also employ the slot limit on certain waters. It is the latter, according to most biologists, that can aid the trophy bass fishery most effectively.

Trophy Catch And Release Rates

The California trend in productivity of bass and of trophy size fish right now is downward, due to shrinking water levels, according to Bottroff. Lakes peak in terms of total populations of largemouth and in terms of trophy production. Those timings are obviously different.

"When a reservoir is low for a period of time and then fills up, we find that it will reach a maximum density in about a year and one-half," says the biologist. "The mean size of bass then increases, and the pounds of fish remain fairly constant. The numbers of very large fish produced from the initial two years of high water will peak out between six and 10 years later. That will be a very dominant year-class for a long time."

Things haven't changed dramatically in California during the past 10 years, though, according to Bottroff. The fishing pressure is very similar. The giants, those over 15 pounds, are still being caught, but now many are finding their way back into their aquatic environment. The biologist places that release figure at between 20 and 30 percent.

"If your goal is to catch a 12 pound largemouth someday, and you do catch a 10 pounder," says Jim Brown, San Diego Lakes Recreation Manager, "then it makes sense to put that fish back. It should increase your chances of catching a 12 pounder, even if you have to catch that fish again."

"I tend to release almost all the bass that I catch," he continues. "I released a 16 pounder that I caught in Lake Hodges and I personally believe in catch and release, but I would not mandate it."

In a recent survey, anglers said they prefer to catch larger bass, like this 15-pound, 7-ounce fish. Fisheries agencies in several states seem to understand those desires in establishing management programs.

Shallow Vulnerability

Over the years, the major population of bass that frequented the easily accessible, shallow, shelf-type feeding areas were caught. The bass that had deeper territories or more secluded territories are the ones that exist today, and many anglers believe that they're just a small segment of what was once our normal bass population.

Old timers report catches like 30 fish over eight pounds in a two-week period, and more than 180 largemouth exceeding eight pounds caught in just six weeks from one Florida river in the early '70s. In their next breath, they point out that trophy bass guides moved into the area and started fishing it regularly.

"Anyone could catch a big fish then," a former guide told me. "All you had to do was go to any bend in the river and throw a shiner with a cork against the hyacinths."

"Sometimes we would catch three at once. We had to be careful about the number of baits we put out, because if a school of bass moved through we would have more action than we could handle. Our lines would get tangled," he recalls. "It's not like that any more."

In Florida alone fishing pressure over the last ten years, and fishing ability, has increased tremendously. Most fishermen are a lot better now. The widespread use of good quality bass boats, depth finders, pH meters, Color-C-Lectors and other sophisticated equipment help anglers become more proficient. Fishermen now have more fishing time, and more interest in being better anglers.

The old adage that 90 percent of the fish are caught by 10 percent of the fishermen may no longer be true. Today, probably more like 20 percent of the fishermen are catching 90 percent of the fish. One out of every five fishermen is now fairly successful.

Probably the most effective way to maintain a quality big bass fishery is to replace the eight pound bass quicker. Right now, in southern waters, it takes 7 to 10 years to replace fish that size in the best of growing conditions. To shorten the replacement time, you have to insure that there are plenty of four to six pound bass, i.e., a 14" to 21" slot limit. With those fish protected, an eight pound bass will be a two or three year replacement resource. Of the one-pounders available, few will make it to eight pounds. If you have 400 one pounders, only one will be left in eight years. Biologists and sport fishermen should not only think in terms of replaceability but also the bass value to the resource.

The giants may be necessary in terms of predator/prey balance to the fishery. An eight-pound bass can accomplish things in an environment that eight one-pound bass can't. She can eat full-size gizzard shad, bluegills, large shiners and all the forage that outgrows the little bass that are left. When the forage base outgrows the predator fish, it is out of control. Many fisheries biologists believe that trophy bass have a purpose in balancing the environment.

Progressive thinking fish and game agencies are utilizing management techniques such as slot limits and size limits on bigger fish. Texas, a state known for great strides in protecting their big bass fishery, recently went to a five-fish, 14-inch minimum length limit. While their bass management policies have set the pace for others, many states in the deep south are slow to implement restrictions that could help save the trophy bass.

7 GENETIC GIANTS

Breeding Goliaths Of The Future

ASK TEXANS WHAT their state's most notable success has been over the past several years and you may get different answers, depending on the person to whom you are speaking. Many freshwater anglers believe it was the introduction of the Florida bass gene by former Texas Parks & Wildlife Department Director, Bob Kemp. That was the significant beginning to the department's rapidly escalating notoriety for genetic experimentation.

Texas' largemouth bass brood fish were initially obtained from Florida during 1971-1973. Stocking efforts started throughout Texas in 1972, and the Florida gene has been introduced into more than 200 public reservoirs. In all cases, the Florida bass gene has become established. P&W studies have shown that Florida largemouth benefit existing bass fisheries by increasing prey utilization efficiency and the range of reservoir habitats occupied.

Kemp, who is now deceased, once told me that favorable cost-to-benefit determinations have been found for the overall program, and that it is successful in providing fishermen of Texas with more recreation and greater sport fish harvest. Increases in existing bass fishery after the introduction of Florida bass have been documented.

Florida bass stockings have been directly responsible for all Texas state records caught since 1980. The old existing trophy mark of 13 pounds, 8 ounces, caught from Medina Lake in 1943 lasted as the state record for 37 years. The northern-strain largemouth was bumped from the Texas Top 50 Largemouth Bass list in March of

63

1989. Those 50 larger bass range up to the existing, and probably soon to be broken, 17 pounds, 10.7 ounces.

The increased production of trophy fish is the result of the faster growth of the Florida bass species and its intergrades, particularly in later years of life. The faster growth of Florida bass compared to the growth of native bass in the same body of water strongly indicates a genetic influence rather than environmental factors being responsible for the observed changes.

Today, experimentation in the area of genetics goes on, and it offers further potential for improving the state's trophy fishing. The P&W Department fortunately is not a conservative organization satisfied with past results. They still seek improvement to the bass fishery and are taking steps to accomplish that. Texas continues its research into potential genetic improvements through stocking of selected strains of bass. Knowing the genetics of a standing population can be altered, the P&W Department biologists are actively searching for ways to achieve maximum benefit for the fishery.

Selective breeding, long used in farming, has merit in fishery management also, according to Dr. Gary Matlock, Director of Fisheries with the P&W Department. The benefits to be derived by Texas fishermen are many: bass that are easier to catch, larger bass and more bass. Selectively breeding such fish may be suitable for certain management situations, such as population control, catch-and-release or trophy-specific waters. They might be valuable for introduction as a population control fish where an over-population of forage exists or in small waters that seldom grow monster bass.

The department staff has set out to determine the most efficient means of selections and which ones actually result in the greatest potential to the fishery. Genetic techniques now available are providing fishery managers with interesting options. Like other experimentation, successful accomplishments and clear understanding of the benefits to anglers take time.

Sex Tinkering

For over four years, the Texas P&W Department has been conducting a three-level experiment on controlling the sex of bass, and it could have a great impact on the quality of fishing. Genetists

It may be possible to clone unusually large Florida bass in the near future. Florida-strain largemouth have an insatiable appetite and a mouth to back up that characteristic.

have developed techniques to establish populations of all-male or, more preferably, all-female bass. This breakthrough in bass genetics first occurred in 1986 at the Heart Of The Hills Research Station.

Hatchery personnel can now easily dictate the sex of bass by feeding newly-hatched fry specific hormone-laced food during the time their sexual organs are developing. The fish develop into normal, functional females capable of reproduction.

There are a number of potential bass management benefits to controlling sex ratios through genetic selection. Females generally achieve three to four times the weight of male bass. Females have shown to be better fitted for survival under adverse conditions and are generally longer-lived. Reservoir stockings of all female bass could lead to better survival and ultimately larger fish.

Reproduction can be increased by adjusting the sex ratio to emphasize females, an especially useful management option for biologists in the initial stocking phase of new impoundments. With their tremendous growth rates and ability to adapt to environmental changes, females only can be stocked into trophy lakes. Bass population average size could be increased without employment of restrictive harvest limits. Single sex production is just the first step, though, in the "genetic game plan."

The second level is production of triploid bass which usually results in increased levels of chromosomes and, as a result, sterility. This is done by temperature (hot or cold) or pressure shocking eggs which causes a 50 percent increase in the number of chromosomes (the bearer of the genes) within the cells. This normally results in faster growth and larger sizes of the individuals.

Triploiding has been used extensively over several years in the production of grass carp. Due to the triploid fish being sterile, food intake is primarily directed at growth. Energy contributed to the reproductive chores of the normal bass in the wild won't be expended by the triploid largemouth. Relieved of the stress of spawning, they become "eating machines" and typically outgrow their counterparts.

The P&W Department began experimenting with egg heat shocking a couple of years ago, but survival was poor. Today, they use a pressure treatment and are having some success. In fact, their biologists produced the first triploid largemouth bass on record in the summer of 1988. Dr. Gary Garrett of the department's Heart Of The Hills Research Station at Ingram said that 14 triploid bass were identified.

The last level in the experiment is cloning, or production of genetically-identical bass by fertilizing eggs without the genetic contribution of the male. In a laboratory situation, the sperm is irradiated to eliminate all genetic contribution to the offspring. Egg fertilization is performed with that gene-sterilized sperm. In other words, the male and its genes are not even needed for female reproduction in this case. Talk about obsolescence!

Benefits of clones would be realized mostly in hatchery breeding programs. That can impact those of us in the "field" though. Largemouth with specific traits such as fast growth, large size, temperature tolerance or disease resistance can be produced for

Tomorrow's bass of a lifetime may come from a test tube, but what's wrong with that? The future of a trophy fishery in most states may rest with the results of genetic research.

stocking into lakes and rivers. In a hatchery, such controlled genes can easily be maintained in subsequent generations of bass.

Once triploiding techniques have been fully developed, it will be relatively easy to produce cloned bass, according to some fishery biologists. Imagine producing exact genetic duplicates of large-mouth over 18 pounds. A more desirable characteristic would be difficult to think of!

Foreign Experiments

Other genetic research to determine which strain is best suited for Texas waters is being conducted by the P&W Department on largemouth bass from Florida, Cuba and California. Future stocking programs may include genetic combinations with characteristics derived from brood stock obtained from such foreign locations.

Although waters in Cuba were stocked with Florida bass over 50 years ago, some differences may have developed, according to Dr. Bill Harvey, Texas P&W Department biologist.

"It was assumed that Cuba grew large bass because of the tropical climate and abundant forage," he says. "That may not be true, because most Cuban lakes are not really tropical in temperature. Most have a comparatively poor forage base, comprised mostly of bluegill. That might indicate that hybrid crosses between Cuba largemouth and other strains will be effective at utilizing this forage in Texas."

Hybridization is viewed as a good management tool, since first-generation crosses between native and Florida bass have shown the best growth characteristics. Also, by crossing Cuban bass with a special group of native bass, biologists will be able to identify stocked bass years after release simply by analyzing a small piece of fin tissue.

The imports from Cuba have been found to differ genetically from both native Texas bass and Florida bass in the state. The original Cuba brood fish were brought to Texas via Mexico in special shipping boxes. Ten small Cuba largemouth spawned at the Tyler State Fish Hatchery in 1985 and 20,000 offspring were shipped to other facilities for study.

Studies to date have revealed that Cuban bass, for example, exhibit excellent growth rates and also spawn prolifically at an early age. In fact, 8- to 10-inch brood fish may produce twice as many fry as a typical Florida bass that size. They also seem to be very aggressive, even at a fingerling stage, and that means, for the angler perhaps, more catches.

Another P&W genetic-type experiment in its early stages is an evaluation of bass with high relative weights (plumpness) as brood fish to produce fingerlings. They would be used for stocking reservoirs from which they were collected. It is believed offspring will be better suited to the multiplicity of environmental factors associated with those reservoirs.

Share A Lunker

Probably the most innovative program involving trophy bass and the future of such a fishery was introduced by the Texas Parks & Wildlife Department in late 1986. Called "Operation Share A Lone

Star Lunker", it provided an opportunity for anglers in that state to be recognized for catching huge bass while allowing the department to use the fish for research and production.

Any bass, legally caught during the period from November 26, 1986 until April 30, 1987 that exceeded 13 pounds and could be delivered in a healthy condition to a hatchery was a candidate. The angler donating his trophy was offered a free mount or having a free fiberglass replica made and releasing the fish alive into a lake within 100 miles of the hatchery. Such tangible rewards are an incentive for the lucky angler to do his share toward assuring the future of trophy bass fishing.

Corporate sponsors became involved at the beginning by providing financial support and assistance in spreading the word of the program. Promotions, posters and wallet-sized cards detailing proper fish-handling techniques were distributed to the public. A toll-free phone number was established to screen and collect information on potential qualifying catches.

Program goals were to try to improve the quality of largemouth bass available in the state, to promote catch and release fishing so that more large fish would be available for anglers to enjoy and to allow Texas fishermen to put something back into their sport. The program had a significant benefit in that it promoted an increased public awareness of conservation. Proper handling and release of trophy bass was stressed, as well as the philosophy behind specific bass restrictions and limits on the various reservoirs.

The genetic improvement program attracted seven lunker bass, all Florida-strain or first generation integrades. They were kept in a giant aquarium at the Tyler Fish Hatchery. The goal of having high-quality brood stock for producing offspring with genetic potential for maximum growth was attained. Visitor attendance at the hatchery increased tremendously with the largest collection of huge bass in captivity being closely observed.

The first entry in the program was the 17-pound, 11-ounce state record bass caught the day before Thanksgiving on Lake Fork east of Dallas. The fish, named "Ethyl", survived a fungus infection and became an exemplary subject. Scale analysis revealed her age as being 10 years and her length and corresponding growth each year.

Although Ethyl was unable to spawn, two of the genetic giants were, producing a total of 20,000 fingerlings for the department brood fish program. All seven fish were paired with Florida-strain male bass and closely observed. The biggest to spawn was a 15-pound, 8 1/2-ounce Lake Fork bass.

"Five or six years ago, I would have mounted that fish," admitted the lucky angler and professional guide, Dennis Canada. "But, to me now, it is more gratifying to have let it go. I just hate to kill a fish that big or any fish!"

Canada's fish was the first "loaner" returned to its home waters. Prior to its release, a radio tracking device was surgically implanted in the bass so that more can be learned about trophy-size largemouth. He later re-caught the fish, and it served a second hitch in the program.

Some of the Operation Share A Lone Star Lunker bass have died in hatchery captivity, but the most have been released into their lakes of origin. The mortality factor appeared to stem from the over-zealous aggression by the males during the spawning process. Big females, at this time of the year, won't put up much of a fight to ward off the smaller males, and in hatchery tanks, they were confined and could not get away from the males. A lot was learned from the program.

Section Two

TECHNIQUES FOR TROPHIES

- **Natural Signs**

- **Deep Water Concentrations**

- **Night Appointments**

- **River Haunts**

- **Top Water Tactics**

- **Cold Crankin'**

- **Weedscape Ways**

- **Shiner Savvy**

- **Jungle Flippin'**

- **Why Big Fish Get Away**

- **Catch and Release**

CHAPTER 8

NATURAL SIGNS

Follow Nature's Roadmap To Big Fish

THE PREVIOUS TWO weeks in Central Florida had been extremely cold with only minimal warming rays from the sun. The skies remained overcast and water temperatures plummeted from the pre-holiday 70's down to the low 50's.

"The only places producing now are the spring-hole areas," said my friend and guide Dan Thurmond. "The water temperature in them is a few degrees warmer and that seems to attract the bass."

The unusually low air and water temperature readings had completely shut down the largemouth bass activity, except for a few select areas known to a handful of die-hard trophy bass anglers. Thurmond is one of the few who remain constantly 'in the know.'

"The surface water temperature on Orange, Lochloosa, Rodman and most of the other Ocala Forest lakes is running 49 to 52 degrees with only a degree or two variation at to 10 or 12-foot depths," said Thurmond. "There are a dozen or so spring holes on Rodman that may produce a big fish," he assured me.

Under ideal conditions, finding the major springs is relatively easy, but conditions are seldom ideal. Low water levels, minimal current flow and no wind are optimal environmental characteristics to search for the presence of a spring that affects a large river or lake area, such as the Lake Oklawaha impoundment, more commonly called Rodman Reservoir by locals.

Springs 'boil up' from a limestone rock and sand strata and their existence is often detected by its "imprint" on the water's surface above the outcropping. The 'boil' above major springs in similar waters is easily noticed unless the wind has roughed the surface. Under normal conditions however, only the observant and experienced "spring hunter" can find them. The angler that knows what to look for can often discover several spring influences.

Thurmond had taken the time to pin-point a half dozen such spots. Our initial casts of huge native shiners at 4 p.m. began a short "check-out" trip at the springs holes. While the first area produced nothing over a period of 40 minutes, a second spring hole turned out to be a productive spot. We each caught a largemouth in the final hour of light. One weighed 6 1/4 pounds and the other 11-pounds, 5-ounces. The fish were tagged prior to their release.

We found out later that a bass tournament that frigid day resulted in a six-pound winning stringer and "big bass" of 2 1/2 pounds! While the 30 artificial lure tossers feverishly worked those waters, none apparently found a bass-laden spring hole.

I fished the same spring area the following morning and landed and released a 7-pound, 2-ounce beauty. On the next morning, Dan guided a party to that hole and another in the same general area and had additional success. His two angling clients caught 10 bass that all weighed between five and 8 1/2 pounds. Eight bass that Dan and his party caught one day later averaged over 6 1/2 pounds. All but two were released to fight another day.

When the water temperature is cold and most bass are sluggish, then it's time to head for the spring-influenced areas. This is obvious to some anglers, others don't take the time to search out those productive spots. A slow-moving shiner is one of Thurmond's keys to making such areas produce in the "dead of winter."

By observing "nature's signs," which reveal ideal bass spots, productive techniques can be utilized to catch trophy largemouth. The finding and catching of trophies from spring holes during winter weather is just one way.

Plant Variations

Other "signs" include plant variations that denote forage availability. For example, not all pad beds are alike in terms of their productivity, a bass guide once told me.

Big bass in the dead of winter often come from the spring holes where warmer water temperatures induce actively-feeding bass.

"There are more insects on plants with overlapping leaves," he explained. "That's why spatterdock and fragrant water lilies are better than lotus or dollar bonnets. Spatterdock, in fact, is best of all because the leaf is above the water and the bugs can light on it."

That makes them more accessible to the forage fish that focus on bug meals. Predators such as largemouth bass naturally follow their prey to such areas. The pad types from one area to another may have a subtle difference, but it is one worth looking for.

Another observation to make while around pads is to look for the tiny holes in the leaves. They reveal where bream, a prime forage for trophy bass, have attempted to suck a bug through the vegetation. This sign is more commonly found on fragrant water lily leaves which lie on the surface of the water.

I learned years ago about bonnet worms, a prime forage of bream. You have to look closely for a tiny hole on top of a pad leaf. The hole at the point of intersection with the stem below indicates the presence of a worm. With forage fish hanging around such pad areas, it's not unusual to find largemouth.

Wood Ways

Smaller, light green trees along a shore usually mean a swampy area, according to a botanist. Taller hardwoods and dark green plant life mean fertile, sandy bottoms. Plenty of experience on the water since has taught me to look for such keys, because that's where the biggest bass can usually be found. Fertile bottoms and vegetation correspond to a healthy food chain, right up to the predator bass.

In reservoirs, the signs may be very noticeable. After a lake bed is flooded, trees that were left uncut for fish habitat reveal a lot about the topography below. By analyzing those types of cover, an angler can tailor his fishing technique for each.

"Hardwoods like oak and maple trees usually grow on the edges of sloughs or ditches," says Lake Conroe, Texas, guide, Zell Rowland. "Softwoods like pine trees will normally be on a flat without a depth break. Trees with a real light brown tint are softwoods; hardwoods will turn extremely dark or even black in the water."

The hardwoods are productive year around, according to Rowland. Fall and pre-spawn spring are the prime times, though, to concentrate on the hardwoods. During the spawn in the spring and on into the summer, he prefers to fish the softwoods. The latter are also early morning spots where fish are coming out of sloughs and moving to the flats to feed.

To find the most productive spots, Rowland looks for a creek channel or ditch bend within the trees. The elevation change of even a small depression on those edges would be a break point that would hold bass, he claims. Most of the year, Rowland prefers to toss a crankbait in the woods.

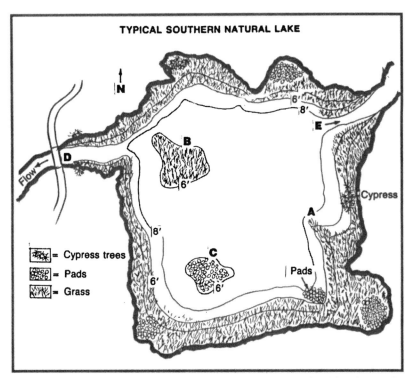

FIGURE 3 - On a typical southern natural lake, numerous signs should lead an angler to trophy bass. Those variances in terrain or habitat type are usually productive spots to fish. In locations A through E, something about each area is different from the rest of the lake.

"Generally, the further back into a creek that you go, the more hardwoods you'll find," he points out. "Those great spring fishing areas will also have larger stumps on the edge of the creek banks. The best pattern then is flippin' those stumps."

When the bass are in trees near a bank, he may use a buzz bait or top water chugger-type bait. In the summer, the better wood angling lies in the deeper creek channels near the main lake body. Worms are his choice then for maximum action in the deeper waters.

Trees, whether in a natural lake or partially submerged in a reservoir, grow in particular places for a reason. Tree lines denote the presence of deeper water, submerged roadbeds or ditches, creek

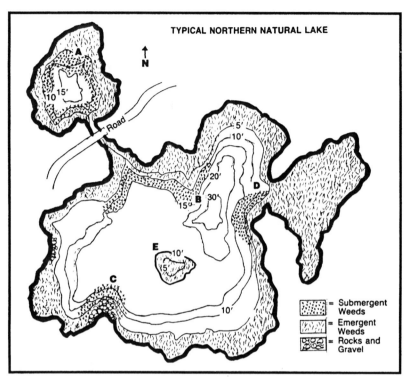

FIGURE 4 - A typical northern natural lake might have additional rocks and more submerged vegetation, but the natural signs exist to lead an angler to bigger bass. Use your eyes and your sonar to pinpoint the productive lunker spots. Notice that the better big bass locations (A through E) are all at the edge of a variance in habitat or bottom contour (or both).

channels, etc. and are excellent surface "keys" to what may lie below. Forage will often move along such structures without penetrating them. Lunker bass await just inside.

Wildlife Cycles Interact With Bass

Watch the skies for heron activity signaling great bass areas. The birds that move en masse at daylight to a menhaden minnow concentration should be followed. The presence of blue herons at anytime usually indicates a prime feeding spot for forage fish, and largemouth won't be far away. The fish-finding birds won't waste time hunting in non-productive waters.

Patches of fog usually denote an area where the water temperature is significantly warmer than surrounding waters. The low light levels bring bass closer to the surface and make them more vulnerable to anglers.

In the deep South, manatees that seek warm waters dislodge plankton and other forage items when they move through an area. Water-wise anglers are alert for the signs and will fish behind the giant plant grazers, keeping a safe distance between the endangered animal and the boat's prop. Carefully following the wake of a sea cow will usually result in a few bass.

"The best combination of aquatic life is turtles, 'gators and frogs," an old-timer who had fished southern waters for decades once told me. "Find them around offshore pads in 10 feet of water, and you will catch fish. They feed after a forage spree by bass."

Shad schools can often be observed on the lake's surface when the wind is minimal. Crankbaits retrieved beneath a school of threadfin may result in a largemouth or two.

I've always been aware of the relationship between bass and their prey. In fact, my first two books, "Follow The Forage For Better Bass Angling - Volumes 1 and 2," dealt with precisely that subject. The importance of locating and observing bass forage cannot be underestimated. Actively feeding largemouth are found in areas of high prey concentrations.

An area of crayfish can often be noted by the tell-tale signs of tiny burrows in the mud, for example. Scan the shallows carefully, and then select an appropriate live bait or artificial. One that closely resembles the predominant forage should work best.

Other keys such as water temperature and pH can be determined in part by nature's signs. For example, patches of fog usually denote an area where the water temperature is significantly warmer than surrounding waters. In the cooler weather, always fish the warmer water. The low light levels caused by intense fog also bring bass closer to the surface and make them more vulnerable to anglers.

Factors of pH can be noted by observing certain signs. Algae blooming during summer weather conditions result in extremely high values of pH. Rain during winter conditions result in extremely low pH levels. Stay away from each. Find fresh, moving water during hot weather, and deep, large water areas in the winter after a downpour fills tributaries.

The age-old signs are, not surprisingly, very accurate. Some guideposts are unique, but they are also productive. Technology has greatly influenced modern bass fishing, but it should be considered as a supplement to nature's signs for optimum fishing success.

CHAPTER 9

DEEP WATER CONCENTRATIONS

Put Your Jig And Spoon In The Depths

EVER CAUGHT A trophy bass from really deep water? For several years, a Montgomery, Texas, angler has been catching limits of heavy largemouth from water as deep as 70 feet on lakes throughout the country.

Professional angler Randy Fite has a philosophy toward finding and catching big bass from the depths. He has found that deep-water angling for bass of all sizes is excellent in both winter and summer, but success has to do with the way bass relate to structure at different times of year.

In hot weather, they will relate more to the gradual slopes because there is less fluctuation of thermal conditions. During the winter, concentrations of big bass are found primarily on severe breaks or changes in depth. When a drastic variance in weather occurs, the fish are able to quickly move deeper to avoid exposure to the "new" conditions.

The key element in determining the effects of the variance is in the forage relationship. During the summer, the nomadic shad move about near the surface, feeding on the plankton spawned by the sun. When winter sets in, the oxygen content at the surface decreases and the baitfish are "driven" to the bottom. Shad will then relate to the deeper vertical structure and the wise cold-weather angler will key in on this.

To fish this structure effectively, Fite relies on his deep-water eyes -- sonar. Through its use, he is able to read and interpret baitfish

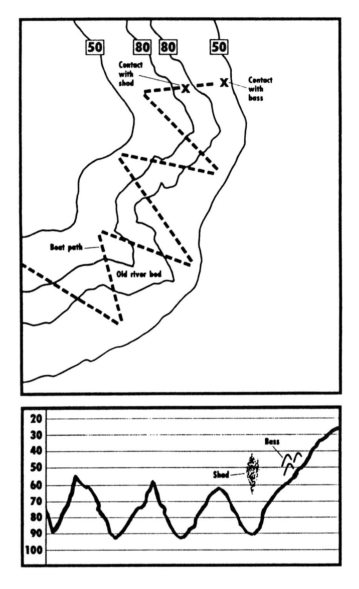

FIGURE 5 - An angler pursuing deep-water bass should run slow, crisscrossing patterns over productive-looking structure (top). He consults his sonar for signs of baitfish or groups of bass. When baitfish are found at a certain depth range (bottom), the angler should then search for bass at nearby structure.

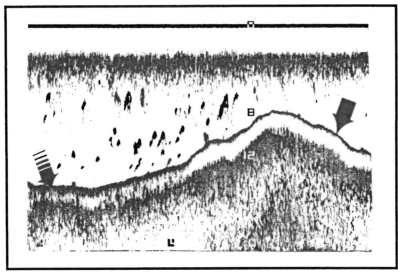

FIGURE 6 - A good sonar unit will reveal the bottom type (soft or hard) present. Soft bottoms (the left half of the figure) may attract several smaller fish, while hard bottoms (the right half) are preferred by the giants.

and bass movements. He then fishes accordingly. Fite feels electronics are essential in finding deep-water bass. According to Fite, when you're fishing in 40 to 70 feet of water, you're looking for concentrations of big fish.

Right after sunup may be the best time to fish deep water. Because shallow-water bass are affected by the sun's rays and bass in the depths aren't, many anglers head for the shallows and fish them for two or three hours; then they begin to probe deeper water. After only a couple of hours of no activity, they give up on deep-water largemouths. Fite contends that this is the wrong approach.

In the summer, Fite usually marks deep-water bass six inches to two feet off the bottom. During the winter, however, the bass will blend into the structure and the angler may have to "draw" them up to chart them, according to Fite. This can be accomplished by catching two or three largemouths from the same good-looking structure. On about the third fish, the spoon won't reach the bottom because the school will actually be bunched up and drawn off the bottom toward the surface--and the descending lure.

Finding concentrations in 50 to 70 feet of water on an LCD or

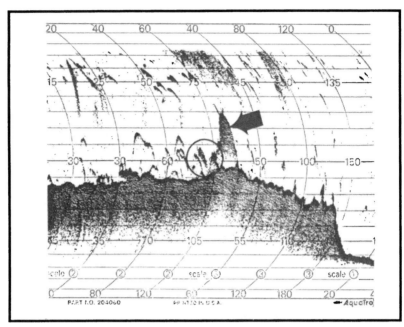

FIGURE 7 - Large bass can often be spotted beneath or to the side of a school of smaller baitfish. The forage appears here as a dense cloud of matter off of the bottom, while three large fish are positioned just beneath (to the left of) the baitfish.

chart recorder is possible only through careful attention to installation and operation details. The transducer should be installed outside of the boat on the stern and it should be sanded with a fine grade of sandpaper for optimal sensitivity.

Wintertime bass concentrations can often be found along deep-water ledges just off a river channel. Underwater points that run into a river channel are excellent bass producers, too. When the bottom of the channel is 80 feet deep, try the lip of the channel, which should be only 55 to 65 feet down. The big bass concentrations move toward the main channels in the tough weather.

"That's why the north end of the impoundment is a good place to find fish," Fite said. "The main river channel is usually the only one with depth. The south end of the lake normally has several major creek channels with the required depth."

Deep-water structure can appear simply as a change in depth, according to Fite. Depth serves the same purpose as brush would in

Largemouth will often relate to sharp drops in depth, and the astute angler with his eyes focused on the sonar will catch them.

shallow normal-colored water. Fite recommends that anglers not overlook brush-less drops in deep water. At 65 feet, bass will get on the structure whether there is brush present or not.

Concentrations of winter bass are more numerous, yet more inconsistent. Summer concentrations may stay in the same spot for several weeks, provided there are no significant weather changes to move them. Fish in the winter may back off and suspend when a cold front passes through. They often disperse until it has passed.

Deep Bait Thoughts

Fite has definite opinions about productive winter baits. He contends that a one-ounce Mann-O-lure is best to cover deeper water faster. The lure is fished vertical to the deep-water fish and is

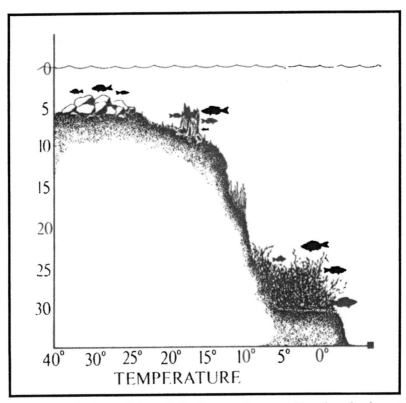

FIGURE 8 - During cold times, lunker bass usually are positioned on the sharpest drops to deep water. Continual cold or hot water temperatures push them deeper.

extremely accurate. Bass can be quickly hooked and put in the boat. The lure can then be dropped quickly to the school for more action.

Early winter fish are usually heavy from feeding on shad during warmer months. They won't move far, so the spoon's motion is important. It should "hop" in one spot for several seconds before being relocated. In cold water, bass can be on structure and yet be dormant. Under these conditions, Fite imparts to the spoon a six-inch hop off the bottom for maximizing his catch.

In deep water with scattered brush or trees, Fite prefers the jig and eel for its weedless advantage. He has caught many big bass on it from depths of 30 to 45 feet! His summer arsenal includes the jigging spoon with a two foot hop, a tail spinner, plastic worms, and smoke-hued plastic grubs. They produce over deep-water structure.

CHAPTER 10

NIGHT APPOINTMENTS

Go After Dark For Monster Prowlers

THE ULTRA-QUIET PERIOD on a cool evening after the heat of the day can convince most trophy size largemouth to forget about daily boat traffic congestion. Big bass in heavily-fished lakes and rivers become less cautious and generally move shallower on their feeding forays when the sun sets. Many anglers realize that, but not too many know just how effective fishing at night can be.

Fishing by moonlight is something that all big bass anglers try sooner or later. Success, though, seldom occurs on one's first nighttime angling trip. The water, and keys to unlocking its largemouth concentrations, are different during the dark part of each 24-hour period.

Waters where particular abilities are necessary under a bright sun take on a different character at night. Methods that produce big bass from such areas during the day may be completely different after dark. Once an angler becomes accustomed to fishing in the dark, and becomes familiar with the best tactics to employ, then he will usually succeed like never before.

The reasons why night angling action is most often productive are many. The fisherman's mistakes are easily covered by the guise of darkness, and that's important for anyone "intruding" into the bass environment. Largemouth are usually less wary after dark, and a normal "fright" response may become "curiosity" then.

My first few nighttime expeditions were trips of frustration. I chose large topwater plugs, made long casts and made them gurgle back to the boat. Explosions in the dark were few and far between, but when they occurred, I would instinctively jerk back on the rod.

Often I had to duck a lure on a projectile course toward my head. Loud noises around a topwater lure that is difficult to see would make anyone nervous. I set the hook and, of course, instantaneously realized that the bass and I hadn't made a connection. Fortunately, I survived, but the experiences were a bit unnerving.

Bass seem to miss their targets more easily at night, or so it seemed. Fishing all night for only four or five strikes is tough to handle. One has to be ready at all times when the lure is wet. There is little opportunity to again attract the fish that has just caught you dozing and made a fool of you. And on those nights when strikes are few and far between, most "daytime" people tend to get very sleepy.

In the summer, though, there is no reason to stop fishing at sundown. In fact, there are good reasons to fish exclusively after dark. I finally discovered them, once I realized that lure selection remains critical, even after dark.

On my fourth nighttime trip, I discovered some of the action that I had always heard about. I had met a man at the boat ramp as I was taking my boat out and he was putting his in. In brief conversation, he related several weeks of exceptional night angling from the lake that I had fished all day and had produced four small bass.

I listened intently as he told of huge catches of giant bass from those waters. Boat ramp talk is usually cheap and I don't usually lend a lot of credence to information from strangers. The following morning, I again ran into the man who was, this time, taking out his boat as I was launching mine. He showed me two bass over eight pounds in his livewell and claimed to have put back 15 smaller ones.

In further discussion, I wrangled an invitation to join him five nights later for some bass action. When we finally were on the water, I was somewhat surprised when he chose a large plastic worm and rigged it Texas-style with the slip sinker and weedless-turned 4/0 hook. I followed suit and began dragging a worm over the underwater structure.

The bass, I learned, could see the plastic wiggler well after dark. It certainly seemed to excite the largemouth population of that lake;

Productive trophy bass angling after dark requires knowledge of bass nighttime behavior and their reliance more upon sound than sight then.

we ended up tired and exhausted the following morning, having caught and released over 25 bass. None were of monstrous proportions, but a couple pushed six pounds.

Worms can be very effective after dusk, but few anglers realize it. Given the maze of obstructions that existed below, a weedless lure was ideal. Hangups with diving plugs can be a problem, but worms, particularly large ones, can probe the depths for the giants. Many anglers put up their worm box at dusk, but they are making a bad mistake!

A great, big bass producer is a black 13-inch worm. One with good bulk to appear a hearty meal is perfect. It also must be thin enough to have great action and ease of setting the hook. Giant plastic baits come in a variety of shapes, and most are very tempting to trophy-size largemouth. Snakes, eels, lizards and waterdogs are just some of the over-sized forms available in plastic. Some shapes don't even resemble a living life form, yet large plastic fare seems to attract its share of big bass.

Most of the giant plastic are most effective after dark when "Texas-rigged" with a light slip sinker and stout 5/0 or 6/0 hook. They are normally retrieved along the bottom and allowed to rest in any crevices or tumble down dropoffs. As the bait comes by stumps

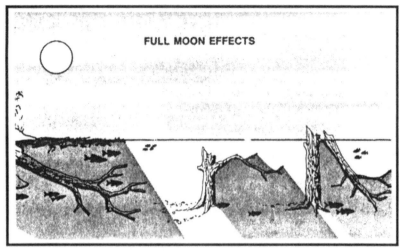

FIGURE 9 - Largemouth become active at dusk and patrol areas bathed in light in search of forage. Some source of light is important for good night angling. Dark areas collect daytime fish, and light areas collect moonlight bass.

or drops off ledges, a strike may occur. Bass of lunker proportions will normally just suck in the big plastic bait.

The size of a productive big bass plastic artificial is, I feel, usually significant. I have always been an advocate of using a mouthful of bait to attract the very biggest bass. Bigger baits just catch bigger fish.

Warm Night Action

Fishing moonlit largemouth haunts is a common occurrence during the summer, when the fish begin to frequent the shallows more often as waters cool after the sun sets. It's then that catching the biggest bass of your life is most possible. Giants of the specie are more accessible to the moon-time lunker hunters than to those working the heated shallows during the day.

If you are not familiar with the areas you intend to fish after dark, though, either hire a guide or pick the waters that you know better. Waters that are not as easy to fish for one reason or another during daylight should be prime spots to consider for a moonlight trip. Good places for a successful nighttime angling adventure usually include the overly-crowded daylight areas.

FIGURE 10 - A full moon casts shadows attractive to bass, and nowhere are they as pronounced as over a white sand bottom. Additionally, places where swimmers frolic attract forage fish to feed on dislodged sediment. Bass are close by.

Popular boating and water skiing waters have just too much traffic during the day, but they can be very productive at night. All large cities seem to have a favorite body of water where jet boats outnumber all other kinds, or where sailing vessels cut constant swathes.

Beach areas loaded with frolicking swimmers often become feeding areas for bass under the cover of darkness. Popular "party" lakes that bustle with fun activities on and off the water all day long are usually overlooked by anglers. Try them at night.

FIGURE 11 - Lights on piers and docks always attract the entire food chain and brush planted beneath many of the structures are an additional invitation to forage fish and predators alike.

Lakes near major metropolitan areas are often crowded with suburbanites during the day. Waters near college towns are prone to attract hoards of water skiers during warm days, as are those areas near large marinas or public parks. Ponds and lakes right in the middle of town that seem to be for public non-fishing use during sunup periods may also have an unexploited bass fishery. Clear water lakes are likely candidates for successful nighttime angling. So are clear, spring-fed rivers, if the angler is very familiar with the currents.

Bass may be very cautious in waters that are normally crystal-clear. Only when the sun's rays do not penetrate the surface due to heavy wave action, cloud cover, or darkness, do most anglers have an opportunity to catch several. The waters may be loaded with giant bass, yet only the highly skilled anglers can entice them to a net during the daylight hours. An experienced night angler may fare far better, however.

A newcomer to night angling trying unfamiliar waters would do best by selecting fishing areas with plenty of lights or landmarks that are visible after the sun sets. He'll need these points of reference to keep from getting lost. The shore-based lights also provide a means to see the action better when nearby. Lighted piers and docks are also extremely productive night areas to fish. The lights attract insects and other small forage, which in turn bring bass to feed. Many of the man-made structures have submerged trees or brush piles near the end, placed there to attract fish.

The alternative is to select a specific night based on the lunar

Glistening moonlit lakes are often productive big bass haunts, particularly those areas with moving waters. Darkness covers the mistakes of anglers, who are better able to capitalize on less wary lunker bass.

phase and not worry about the lake chosen or what lights may be available around its shores after dark. Obviously, the full moon provides the maximum amount of illumination, and that's nice when you are casting to overhanging trees or fighting a fish.

At night, bass will use the same feeding routes that they swim during the day. Just how far they will travel usually depends on light, food and the nature of the structure that guides them. After dark, the movement generally terminates closer to the shallows than in the daytime. Drop-offs near the shallows with adjacent deeper waters are prime nighttime targets for productive anglers.

White, sandy beaches can be very productive spots, since swimmers' feet kick up bottom sediment that attracts baitfish. Bass follow the forage into the feeding shelf and have a better observation chance with the sand acting as back-lighting. Similarly, large pier houses and boat sheds that are painted white or light colors are used by bass. Largemouth will seek some source of light background to enable them a better view of their prey, and most white walls near the surface of the water will aid in their foraging.

Long bars and submerged points in shallow, clear waters are excellent areas to find congregated bass. Any daytime action in such an area probably occurs at the end of the bar. At dusk, the fish may again be near the tip of the bar, but as night sets in, fish movement generally takes place along its sides and possibly onto a feeding flat located closer to shore.

Trophy bass are active in shallow areas at night but few anglers go after them. Even less take the time to learn how to catch a giant, leaving more for those of us that stick with it.

CHAPTER 11

RIVER HAUNTS

Don't Neglect Lunker Bass In Moving Water

BIG BASS, SNUG in their habitat, are lazy. Trophy largemouth in rivers are no different. They realize that it's hard to strike at a forage fish in open water and connect. The prey often escapes the pursuit of a lunker in deep channels; there is little to limit the movement of a fleeing baitfish.

River monsters will move a little to feed, but not far. They prefer an area with some current that will wash forage to them, according to guide Bob Stonewater. An ideal feeding area would be a sand bank two feet deep that drops to ten and then gets shallow again. Largemouth can lie in the deeper trough and move onto the feeding grounds to pin the prey against the bank. To be successful at catching the king-size bass from feeding areas takes a certain degree of knowledge, and sometimes, patience.

"You may have to work a prime river area four or five times each day to be successful," says Stonewater. "A big fish will eat a mouthful and then lay back. It might not feed for another whole day. You just can't predict when that lunker will feed".

In 30 years of river fishing, Stonewater has learned much. The guide has learned to identify areas with the highest fishing potential, and his experience is the basis for the analysis.

"You have to know where the current hits, where the dropoffs are, and how the structure sits on the bottom," advises Stonewater. "You must determine how the bottom slopes and where the current turns. That's where the submerged trees will pile up."

Bob Stonewater has learned the ways of a river by spending thousands of days on the St. Johns. He's caught hundreds of trophy bass from river haunts.

Stonewater learned the "ways of a river" by just being on one for years. He did not have a depth finder for a long time, and even today seldom uses his flasher. While much of his experience is a result of thousands of days on Florida's St. Johns River, the knowledge he has developed is applicable anywhere.

How this guide with hundreds of king-size bass to his credit 'reads' a river should be of use to "river rats" all over the country. His ideas about seasons and timing may be unique to many anglers, but they are backed by proven experience. Stonewater is a big bass river guide, pure and simple.

Throughout the day, he'll verify depths with his seven foot rods by poking downward through stained water to reach the bottom. If the tip touches just before the reel is submerged, the affable 43-year

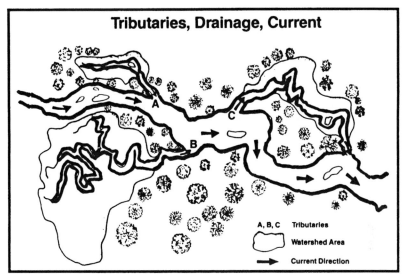

Tributaries, Drainage, Current

A, B, C   Tributaries

    Watershed Area

    Current Direction

FIGURE 12 - At points A, B and C, there are several factors that should be considered in the selection of the prime big bass area. If the water is high, there will be a good flow at C. During low water, the flow may be nil at that point. Areas A and B have an incoming current, denoting the angle these tributaries enter the main channel. They drain a large watershed and should have a more constant flow through the seasons. Rainfall well upstream from where you fish can also affect the flow.

old will call that "reel deep." And, that is deep enough for the lunker bass he's after.

The Right Spot

Stonewater and his clients have caught nine bass over 13 pounds from the St. Johns. But in order to accomplish such feats (even on a smaller scale in other waters), he feels that the angler has to work a long portion of river. In his guide duties, Stonewater will fish a 150-mile stretch. He doesn't fish just one spot. Since he releases most of the bass caught, Stonewater feels that it's important to move about.

"You cannot concentrate on one area and catch 600 bass over 10 pounds from it," he points out. "The fish just won't be there. You need several good spots all along a river."

His 'perfect' spot would be a deep creek that is flowing into or leaving a river channel. A quick drop off on each side of the point, down to 12 feet of water, is ideal. The deep water right up to the bank allows a trophy bass to trap the forage against it. Weed patch cover extending 3 or 4 feet out from the shoreline, and eel grass nearby on the inner bend of the river in three to four feet of water would make for perfect habitat, according to Stonewater.

Many people have a hard time realizing how a little ditch off the main river channel can hold a big fish. Anglers won't generally go into places that are only ten feet wide, but the lunker bass will.

Feeding Holes

Vegetation growing out over water is great cover for a big bass. A cut bank or quick drop at the shore makes such habitat ideal. A lunker can chase a forage fish right up underneath the surface-bound weeds and the prey cannot get away.

When the water is shallow beneath the vegetation, a lunker bass can only swim into it so far and remain wet. The angler can be fishing an area so shallow, the bass will never have a chance to get at the lure or bait. If an angler is using a live shiner, that baitfish looks for such places because it knows to stay out of the deep water.

"If a big bass has to work too hard for a forage fish, it may just go back down into a hole and wait for another attempt," Stonewater points out. "River bass don't like to waste their energy. As they get older and bigger, the lunkers will figure out easier ways to feed!"

Whenever it rains and the water flow increases in the river or tributaries, Stonewater looks for those natural feeding holes with current. A lot of new bait is washed into the river and it's hugging the shoreline tightly as it washes downstream. When forage gets trapped on the deeper river banks, it can seldom escape a big bass.

Some creeks or outlets have flowage at certain times, such as high water periods. On one fishing excursion with Stonewater, we pulled into a small ditch off a main river channel. The water, no wider than 15 feet or so, had a significant current moving through it. The eight foot depth, sharp sloping shoreline and aquatic vegetation on the banks made this spot ideal.

The current seemed to be moving into the tributary however, and I was puzzled. We were far from any tidal effects, and there had not been a heavy rain far upstream which might cause such an occurrence. The ditch was actually a fork of the main river that only

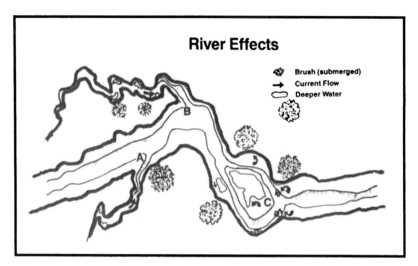

FIGURE 13 - A creek entering a main river channel at a deep outside bend (B) has a more profound effect on largemouth habitat than a creek coming in along a stretch (A). Trophy bass fishing should prove best where deep intersects deep (point B). Knowing the depth and direction of current can tell an angler where the chances of finding a brushpile and big bass are best. Point C is where the current bends abruptly and an eddy helps to contain submerged logs floating down river.

flowed during relatively high waters. The small channel is dry in places downstream during normal water levels and no flow exists then. It was just a case of knowing the ways of that river.

We fished that morning together and caught and released four big bass (weighing around 22 pounds) from a couple of guide Stonewater's favorite spots. On another abbreviated trip one year earlier, we had two largemouth of bragging size. They totaled 17 pounds and came from similar locations, miles away. On still another trip with the river guide, my wife, Lilliam, caught her largest ever bass, an 8 1/2 pounder.

Baiting Up

When the big bass are ready to feed, Stonewater is usually ready. He uses both artificial and natural baits over the prime river habitat. Live shiners are extremely effective for the guide and a majority of his (and clients) trophy largemouth were fooled by the forage fish.

A small quiet river can yield huge largemouth, like this 15-pounder. You have to know where to look for the giants, however, and what lures and baits may fool one.

Fishing the big live baits has taught Stonewater some concepts that are productive when applied to plugs. Big forage fish give off slow vibrations when moving through current, notes the guide. Big crankbaits often have a slow wiggle, producing similar sound waves.

Small, tight-wiggling lures catch small river bass, he points out. Big bass go for large lures. In fact, in one month, the guide and clients caught seven bass ranging from 7 to 10 3/4 pounds on Killer "B 3's". Over the same period, their shiners accounted for 27 large-mouth which scaled from 6 to 11 1/4 pounds. The live baits caught about four times as many lunkers. Those percentages (shiner vs. artificial) are fairly typical in river waters that Stonewater fishes, regardless of the season.

River bass throughout the country have favorite habitat to feed on. There are very little differences between the Florida bass and the northern-strain when it comes to selecting an area in the river for foraging. Learning to identify those with the best big bass potential is well worth the trouble.

CHAPTER 12

TOP WATER TACTICS

Surface Fare Entices The Giants

THE ADRENALIN FLOWS when a huge largemouth charges your topwater plug and simply boils at it. Most anglers will wait for the bass that misses its strike to return to a stationary plug. They'll simply let that surface plug sit. If the fish does not come back after it on the next twitch, another cast to the same area may generate the strike.

At certain times of the year - spring and fall (winter in the deep south), and at certain times of the day - low light times during hot weather and high light times during cold weather), trophy-size bass may be more active in near-surface waters. Topwater fare is often the best attractant for giant largemouth, if your heart can take the excitement.

When a huge bass misses the plug, one effective ploy is to immediately throw a second lure to the fish before it has time to leave the area. The bass will usually come up on a "re-introduced" topwater plug and try to decide whether or not to kill it. Pick up a second rod rigged with a sinking or descending bait even and toss that.

Throw a second lure right back on top of the fish instantly, and you'll catch most of those fish. If you are fortunate to have a couple of rigs lying beside you, then you could toss a completely different lure at a striking bass. In fact, many anglers rely on the ploy whenever they're getting "short strikes" on any type of topwater plugs. If a bass hits behind the bait, throw a different one immediately to that spot. You'll generally catch the fish.

Big bass that feed actively on top are often difficult to find, but a few techniques are successful at locating and catching more. Hungry largemouth may come up and smash a topwater bait, but bass are not always hungry. More times than not, it may take some encouragement from the angler to entice the strike.

Bass may be oblivious to what is going on overhead, where minor commotions neither scare nor attract the predator. At other times, they'll bolt toward the object on the surface and 'boil' the lure, missing it completely. The trick to productive topwater angling is to be ready at all times and know the tricks that may give you an edge over the near-surface bass.

Too much ruckus may be the turn-off. Some successful anglers will file down the lower lip of a chugger-type surface baits so that it won't gulp so much water as it's twitched. Less disturbance in calm, clear waters is often more productive. In the same vein, cutting lips off buoyant diving plugs converts them to top water baits and allows their moving through the water while emitting less "noise."

A lure with minimal action can attract fish under the right conditions. Some anglers twist propeller blades of a prop bait in the opposite direction to make them turn easier. The easier the blades spin, the less noise given off and the more productive they are at times. Still others will snip off the front hook on each treble to make the plug more weedless. They'll fish it in heavier cover with added assurance of few hangups and a smoother "ride" back to the rod tip.

Another trick to draw a return visit from a "short striker" is to crank the bait hard. Instead of letting a plug sit after a missed-strike, quickly reel it away in an "escape" mode. In the underwater environment when a small panfish has a near catastrophe encounter with a bigmouth, such behavior results. It will pull all stops to vacate the area in a big hurry, and a bass may just go for the reeling bait.

If that ploy doesn't work, try retrieving the surface plug slowly underneath the water to entice a strike. The action may draw an impulse strike. Larger bass, in particular, may hit a prop-type bait quicker if you pull it barely under the surface than if you leave it on top. They won't explode on it like they might with other types of

FIGURE 14 - An erratic, skitter-type plug is usually very productive when used in clear waters. Bass need to be able to see the change in movement to strike it, though. An erratically-retrieved plug in muddy waters may generate several swirls and misses, but the bass will seldom connect.

topwaters being pulled fast. They'll just come up and suck it under.

Often, you may have to "wait out" a bass that has missed the plug. Rather than rip the topwater plug away or leave it sit and cast a second offering, a third option exists. And that is doing nothing. The chances are good that the fish is still observing its "prey". Let the lure sit for a good three or four minutes before twitching it.

The bigger the bass, the longer the plug should remain motionless, while it makes up its mind whether or not to eat the plug. Often

103

Fooling a giant bass, like this 15 pounder, on a small top water plug is always exciting. Guiding such a lure around heavy cover takes practice, to prevent snags.

in the fall, the less you move the bait, the better off you are. Drawing surface strikes from our quarry with this ploy takes patience and persistence, but it is an exciting form of aquatic enjoyment.

Varying the "standard" techniques to entice a top water encounter may require an escaping prey tactic or the mortally-wounded ploy. It's hard to know just what mood a bass may be in. He might be playful, hungry or mad, or even a combination.

Regardless of motivation, the fact is that topwater tactics with a variety of lures can be deadly on big bass. When the bass are looking skyward, that's the time for surface fare. Some of my largest fish were enticed to explode the tranquility of my thoughts and the water's surface.

Dedicated anglers have even carved their own topwater plugs to fool bass and derive additional satisfaction. I carved two or three versions of my own surface plug years ago. One in particular was unique in that the lure had a worm trailer that was free to dance

A weedless spoon can usually entice big bass from structure lying five to seven feet beneath the surface. A surface-worked lure will bring the bass to the top, making it easier to keep the bass head up and out of the entanglements below.

behind the plug. I caught some fish with the bait. Homemade models are still being carved today when seemingly every lure design has already appeared on the tackle shop shelves.

Plastic fare that swims across the surface can be extremely productive. A floating worm rig emits vibrations as it "swims" across the surface and can be productive in a variety of waters. In clear water, the long plastic wiggler can be worked above seven and eight feet of water; in darker waters, two or three foot depths appear favorable for enticing big bass.

Weeds hold fish, but some emergent varieties prevent a slip-sinker worm rig from working effectively. That's where the floating worm rig may come into the picture. Even if submergent weeds are within a couple of feet from the surface, this rig can produce, regardless of the bottom depth. Floating worms are effective over hydrilla, which can grow right up to the surface, or over eel grass, which never quite makes it.

A plastic body, slightly tapered to the end of the tail curl, makes for an ideal worm. The prime rig consists of a 12-inch long, high-buoyancy worm or plastic snake on a 4/0 Tru-Turn long-shank hook. No weight is used on the rig so that it remains on the surface as it is retrieved to the boat. The weight of the worm is enough for casting purposes. The best floating worm coloration is snake hue.

Surface buzz baits have always been a favorite of lunker hunters. Best conditions for their use are under cloud cover and over dense vegetation with plenty of isolated holes. A unique, but very effective bait is the in-line spoon/buzz blade; it'll buzz right across the top of the grass. When you get to the holes, you can slow it down to wobble just like a spoon. The buzz blade and spoon must be properly matched.

The regular in-line buzz bait will run through this terrain well, but will not easily attract a bass if you drop it into a hole. Most in-line buzz baits do not resemble forage once you stop them. This spoon combination, though, will wobble down if you drop it into a hole. This combination falls just like a spoon, so you can wobble the bait slowly through the hole and then break out on top and buzz it on to the next hole.

Surface-buzzing spinner baits generally have a blade design that pops it up on the surface and allows the fisherman to crank it back at a very slow pace, keeping it on top at all times. Used around dense grass patches such as pepper grass, sawgrass and eel grass, buzz baits are normally fished with the rod tip held high.

The angler should begin reeling just before the lure hits the water so that it is on the surface always. The baits are effective in both pockets and on the point of weed beds. The retrieve should usually be slow, but can be speeded up to trigger bass into striking.

The strikes normally occur just after the lure has bumped the piece of structure above the bass. Two elements that make the baits successful are noise and contact. Sound is especially important in stained or roily waters, since visibility could be minimal. The main attractor under these conditions requires the right sound. The lures must be emitting sound and be making contact with emergent cover where bass may be staying.

Why largemouth strike such a surface offering can be difficult to figure out. What motivates them to slam a topwater bait on the fringe of their environment is not easy to establish. Certainly, the action and looks of an artificial may command the response of the bass. Often he'll miss his target and come back. Those are the ones I'm after!

CHAPTER 13

COLD CRANKIN'

Bump Up A Big Bass This Winter

THE WEATHER WAS brutal. Snow had fallen and covered the ground for the first time in the history of Welaka, Florida. Yet, some 250 tournament bass fishermen from around the U.S. had braved the harshest elements ever found in that part of the state to fish.

I was one of the die-hards that shrugged off the two inches of snow in the bottom of my boat and the temperature that had fallen from the low 40's into the teens overnight. There were largemouth to be caught, cold front or not.

What followed would not surprise many. Most of the area's bass came down with "lock jaw" and over 100 of the hardy anglers went fishless during the three-day, harsh late-January weather. In fact, only five anglers caught more than seven pounds a day. That's tough fishing for the St. Johns River.

Most anglers tossed reputedly cold-weather baits such as Texas-rigged worms, jig and eels and deep spinnerbaits. The majority of big bass, however, including my only one, were taken on crankbaits. Most of the leaders worked small, chrome Deep Baby "N" along the warm, deep waters of Dunn's Creek, a St. Johns tributary.

Apparently, a few heavyweight largemouth were active as water temperatures in the nearby lakes and the large St. Johns River basin dropped into the almost unheard of upper 30's. The outer bends of Dunn's Creek held warmer moving water and bass, and steadily-reeled crankbaits seemed to be the secret weapon.

This 16-pound, 14.6-ounce largemouth was taken from Lake Pinkston in Texas on a crankbait. Cold water in the spring doesn't seem to affect all giant pre-spawn bass.

Crankbaits have normally been considered a fast bait for active fish, one that is tied on during warm weather. The few stringers of big bass weighed in at that event changed my mind as well as that of most participants. Today, my all-season tackle box is adequately equipped with a variety of both the plump and thin-shaped crankbaits.

There is no better "discovery" bait. The crankbait will allow an angler to cover water quickly and often determine productive, unseen structures below. The vibrating baits and the more common crankbaits with large diving lips can be used to check out potential holding areas. Often they will locate submerged stumps and brush, weedbeds or other bass cover.

They'll produce largemouth from the "finds" too. I once caught and released a dozen bass in less than two dozen casts from a small 100-square-foot area. In frigid weather again, my Big "N" crankbait had located a mussel bed, bringing in the evidence on the first cast, and the proof of largemouth on the second. The winds pushed white

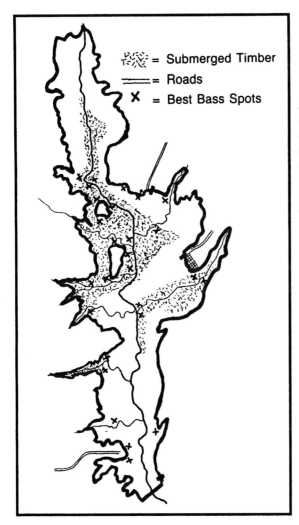

= Submerged Timber

= Roads

X = Best Bass Spots

FIGURE 15 - Prime big bass crankbaiting areas are usually on an elevation change, and often, it lies in conjunction with another type of structure.

caps across the shallow flats and dropped water temperatures, but did not deter the bass. They were stacked up over the warmed floor of shellfish in three feet of water.

The productive trophy bass angler often needs to slow the retrieve in cooler water. A twitched buoyant crankbait can be effective in cool spring time water temperatures for pre-spawn fish. After the cast, wait about ten seconds before giving the lure the slightest twitch. Patience is a virtue here.

109

My parents and I quickly caught a limit of Minnesota pre-spawn bass on the season's opening day years ago. We moved shallow running crankbaits just enough to dimple the surface over eight feet of 50-degree water. The bait action was slow, but that of the largemouth wasn't. We caught several bass over five pounds and culled numerous 3-pound bass that afternoon.

Crankbait System

A successful crankbaiter should have not only a variety of tools (baits) but also knowledge of several productive lunker techniques. Another near-surface erratic retrieval method that has gained quite a cold-weather following is called "jerking." Similar to the twitch, the primary difference is in the force exerted through the rod. The rod action could be likened to jigging a crankbait.

The most effective submergent retrieve is one that keeps the crankbait in regular contact with something. In timber, they should come through the area like a "blind bull" to draw maximum strikes. A crankbait that is intermittently bumped into stumps is one that bass perceive as vulnerable.

Another variation of the timber bump-pause-run method is to pitch a long-billed crankbait into the middle of a brush top, reel in down into the heart of the wood, and then, by slowly raising the rod tip, pull the lure out through the limbs. Deep divers are preferred for this, due to their quick descent and almost snag-free bill protection. The bait will bounce around the obstructions, normally.

Some weed-crankin' techniques, such as the stop-and-go retrieve, will produce bass when used on almost any structure. Once the bait has encountered the vegetation, pause the retrieve and the lure will float toward the surface. Repeat the sequence until a bass interrupts.

A different set of conditions exist in weed crankin' and are not encountered by a wood fisherman. Aquatic plant growth can be tough to pull a lure through, but fortunately most weeds existing during the colder months are not as clinging. In the early spring, tender new growth can be separated from the mass if contact occurs. In either case, the lure can be effectively 'ripped' through sparse plant tops.

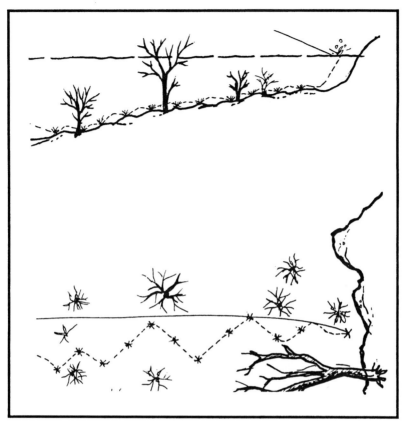

FIGURE 16 - To catch lunker bass, a crankbait should make contact with either structure or the bottom to trigger a trophy fish into striking the bumping bait.

Ripping or raking the bait along deep, submerged structure is also productive. Fast reeling and bumping is what triggers the jolting strikes from big bass. High speed reels capable of 5 to 1 retrieve ratios (or more) are used to "burn" the crankbait back to the boat.

Depth Penetration and Control

The "kneel-and-reel" method is often a good means of keeping your bait in the "fish zone." When that area lies deeper, the successful angler will reach out, or down in this case, to get to them. Long, 7-foot rods are thrust into the water to allow the lure greater descent. The kneeling angler will gain another three to five feet in depth and keep his bait in front of more deep-water bass.

The long two-handed rods are ideal for all crankbait fishing. With them, the angler can cast the bait further and can provide additional hook-setting leverage from placing the butt along the arm or against the stomach. For maximum depth the bait should be "tuned" to run perfectly straight on the retrieve.

Crankbait depth can be controlled. They can be "tuned" to run right or left and thus shallower. Simply, bend the screw eye in the opposite direction that you want it to run. This is an advantage when fishing certain structure such as piers or fence rows.

The biggest deep-running crankbaits are my favorite lunker bass catchers. I've proved the effectiveness of big baits for big bass often over the years. Long ago, I was on a lake where schooling bass activity centered around a one hour time slot just prior to sundown. The schools of giant largemouth moved along underneath roving masses of shad and 'cut' into them, seemingly without provocation.

My two fishing partners that day began angling for the late afternoon surface feeders with Texas rigged worms, while I chose a Norman Deep Big N. The deep running plug with a Tennessee shad finish has always been super productive for me on big bass under a variety of conditions.

The bass that day were foraging on threadfin shad and the similarly-coated lure certainly did its job. I caught and released two dozen thick-shouldered bass in one hour of fishing, as my partners managed less than 10 small fish between them on their worm rigs. Most of my largemouth caught on the big crankbait would have weighed over three pounds, while my friends' smaller baits produced only a few one pound fish.

That particular Deep Big N closely resembled the coloring of the forage that swam near the lake's surface, It fooled the larger bass who were following below. The large shad bait moving through the same depths as the smaller lures seemingly offered the bigger bass a mouthful and, thus, outproduced the others.

Trolling Tactics

Huge, weighted crankbaits have been used for a dozen years or so in California to catch their Florida bass transplants from deep

Crankbaits come in a variety of natural finishes, as well as in combinations of 'maximum visibility' hues. Selection for giant largemouth is usually based on forage available or Color-C-Lector readings.

water. Lunker hunters even modified their standard lures to prowl the bottoms of San Diego Lakes - with success. Greater depths can be reached, and correspondingly deeper bass, even with trolled crankbaits right out of the box.

Trolling the baits has paid off for me many times. Selecting the right lure that would resemble the lake's primary forage, the thread-fin shad, and run at just the right depth to touch the tops of the submergent hydrilla was the key. The effective depth can be adjusted by reeling in or letting out more line. Maximum depths are normally reached by lures trolled back 150 feet or so. A troller can have his bait in the fish zone longer than a caster who has to contend with the descent and ascent of the lure from the surface.

It wasn't long ago that my 74-year-old mother caught her largest bass ever, a 7 1/2 pounder, on a crankbait trolled past a bed of hydrilla. Three or four minutes of battle ensued after the strike as 100 yards of line were reduced to a few feet. I netted her fish and took pictures before releasing it. That day, several other largemouth up to 6 pounds were taken by my father, who in his 80's, was overjoyed with the trolling passes.

I didn't have a rod out that day, but I did later when my brother went looking for his largest ever. The 7 1/2 pound bass that I caught on our first pass over some deep drops would have been his best, had the fish gone after his crankbait. It wasn't long after that when a magazine editor friend caught a 10 pound plus largemouth from my boat as we trolled along an embankment that had brush scattered along the bottom.

Effective crankbait trolling is not simply a matter of letting out lures and motoring around a lake. To be successful, the angler has to be concerned with motor speed, lure depth (and size), water depth, changes in topography, vegetation, wind direction and speed, structure available, potential hangups, and trolling tackle. Trolling shallow, highly vegetated waters is often very difficult. Frequent snags or weed 'catches' can be frustrating, but anglers with an inordinate amount of patience will find a virtually untapped 'gold mine'.

There are ways to maneuver around potential hangups, but to be successful, the bass troller has to stay near them. Bass will often hang tight to cover, making their strike zone difficult to hit unless the lure tracks nearby. Wind and vegetation may dictate the productive approach. Often, largemouth will hit the lure when presented from only one direction.

Speed is a variable, and the motor should be able to handle from extremely slow up to four or five miles per hour. For pulling crankbaits and maximizing the coverage fast, the gasoline motor is ideal. A key to producing several strikes with an outboard is being able to cover the same area at the exact speed. An essential piece of equipment for the productive troller is a good sonar unit, and unless you know the waters intimately, marker buoys are helpful.

114

CHAPTER 14

WEEDSCAPE WAYS

Probe The Surface Blanket For Trophies

MY PARTNER HAD just asked how any bass was going to see the weedless plug that I had cast onto the top of the duck weed cover. I scooted it ten feet over the compact canopy until the rubber lure settled into less densely-packed vegetation. I twitched the plug, moving it three inches, and was about to answer when a small 'hole' developed in the cover four feet away. The 'hole' quickly closed as the miniature plants settled back into it, but that fish had given itself away.

When the Top Dog was twitched again, the seven pounder exploded on it, weeds and all. I applied steady pressure and led her from the snag-infested water beneath the floating cover. The largemouth leaped skyward twice, showering us with tiny duck weed plants on its final boatside effort to escape the steel in her jaw. I released her to swim back into the darkness beneath the floating cover.

While my first bass from that cove full of duck weed was sizable, several larger ones since then have made such unique cover a favorite of mine. Regardless of the size of the fish, when a bass pops a lure on top, the weed is easily airborne. Such action is always exciting.

It's almost like fishing virgin territory when you "plow" the boat through duck weed to reach a distant pocket in the flooded forest. The trolling motor encounters resistance, but the prop can't become clogged. It lies well below the surface cover.

Largemouth don't seem to be overly concerned about any type of floating blanket. Duck weed, commonly found in most states throughout the country, is one cover that's usually right in the middle of the action. When a big bass explodes on the surface and wraps her jaws around a plug, she'll launch tiny green "specs" everywhere.

Bass are accustomed to seeing air-breathing forage trying to walk over duck weed. Thus, a vital characteristic for a lure to entice bass that live under the stuff is that it must have action on top, yet be visible from below. Curious largemouth will want to see what is making the commotion. A lure dipping through the canopy is an attraction that few bass can resist.

Burke's Top Dog with giant 5/0 double hook on its tail and unique ball-head wire guards protecting the points, is ideal for pulling big bass from the duck weed. It is shaped for going through the surface 'blanket' without gathering an exorbitant amount of debris. The lure has a weighted beam which helps it drop below the layer of green stuff. The rear-end exposure attracts big bass.

Most anglers will eventually discover a cove of duck weed if they visit many lakes. While it may not be found in some areas, at least one species of duckweed exists in most states, and it's a fantastic find for those able to unlock its treasures.

Another big bass technique is dropping a heavy, weedless spoon through the stuff. Retrieve it just below the green blanket allowing the lure's nose to periodically dimple the surface. Bass seem to explode on the spoon as it ascends to the surface every foot or two.

Vegetation Value

Floating plant masses, such as duck weed, lettuce, water hyacinths, and water fern, provide prime cover for trophy largemouth. Protection from non-aquatic predators and a sense of security is what attracts the bass to the unique environment. They can roam freely beneath the nomadic canopies in search of prey.

The value of floating aquatic plants for producing and maintaining quality fisheries is well recognized. Vegetation is a significant part of that base in many states with fertile waters.

"The productivity of a body of water is tied directly to the vegetative communities," says Florida Fresh Water Fish and Game

FIGURE 17 - An effective retrieve through the submerged brush should resemble a forage fish trying to swim through, or crawl out on top of, the duckweed. The "walk-the-dog" tactic will usually draw a strike as the lure settles back beneath the canopy, prior to its reaching open water.

biologist Phil Chapman. "Floating plants are generally very beneficial to a fishery. Only if they propagate to a point where the entire lake surface is covered will there be problems. In such cases, there will be a drop in dissolved oxygen."

Chapman cautions, however, that the destruction or wholesale slaughter of floating plant masses is a much more prevalent problem. With the loss of the surface canopies, productivity of the water usually suffers. Prime predator and prey habitat vanishes, and so does the fishing!

Fortunately, areas with extensive floating cover exist and are literally neglected by fishermen. Most anglers will either totally avoid the profuse vegetation canopies, or will simply work the edges. Casts to the weed line may result in a few bass, but the majority of fish, and the larger ones, are often back in under the stuff.

Canopy Types/Distribution

Floating cover is found in most states. The aquatic canopies are either floating-unattached, and floating-attached types. Both groups provide excellent habitat for the largemouth bass, and certain species within each vegetation type are ideal for angler success.

The floating unattached plants drift in a lake or river, with most of the plant body above the water's surface. Roots generally hang free, and such plants are easier to fish. Attached plants that float include many varieties. Their leaves are on the surface, but their roots are anchored in bottom or bank soil. While various forms of water lilies fall into this category, the most desirable plants to the angler are those that have an open water expanse below a mat, without vertical stems. Such vegetation is easier to fish, making special techniques more productive.

Other species of aquatic plants that were once rooted, as well as purely floating ones, exist 'locally' on certain waters around the country. Many agencies responsible for managing aquatic vegetation have performed plant surveys which list acreage by species. Contact your state's Department of Natural Resources or nearest fisheries office for information on the availability of floating bass habitat in your area.

Any time you discover some surface vegetation with adequate room underneath for a large bass, fish it. It really doesn't matter what plant-type it is, you may have found your hot spot!

Effective Big Bass Patterns

General fishing techniques and lures will seldom reach bass under the canopies. Several factors, such as lake-bottom characteristics, weather, and forage availability, affect selecting the best lure and establishing a productive pattern. Fishermen that learn how to fish such cover do extremely well. Most effective patterns in waters containing floating vegetation are based on a quiet approach and careful casting. The lure caster has to accurately hit openings formed in the heavy weedscape or get the lure far back in or under the cover.

Bass are usually located along wind-blown shorelines, and those that contain a floating weed blanket of any type, are prime spots for lunkers. Cover that extends 8 to 10 feet out from the bank over brush habitat is optimal. This can occur where plants like parrot's feather or pennywort may spread from their roots implanted at bankside, out along the surface. Without adequate top cover though, even submerged timber won't hold bass over extended periods.

This 17-pound, 4-ounce giant hit a yellow-green skirted spinnerbait as it fell from a clump of maidencane into 8 feet of water. Trophy bass often frequent dense vegetation.

It's extremely important to select an artificial or live bait that is appropriate for the weed cover being fished. Tossing every weedless lure that appears potentially productive is not the answer. Lures too light to drop through the floating canopy foul easily and should be relegated to less densely-packed weeds near open water. Few bass are willing to pop through the surface at an unknown intruder moving along on top of the 'blanket'. But give them a glimpse of the potential forage, and watch out!

Lures that can be worked beneath the cover, or through it with some visibility, are best producers. One of the reasons, too, may be that bass seem to hang on to a lure longer when it falls or runs under a weed 'security blanket'. They'll hit the bait harder in the darkened environment, seemingly without cause for alarm.

Texas-rigged worms are productive in most types of floating cover, only if the sinker is pegged and heavy enough to punch a hole

119

in the weed mat. If the cover is too intertwined for line tension to 'cut' through the weed blanket on the retrieve, the angler is relegated to casting into holes and pockets. Ideally, the worm can be crawled over underwater structure without significant line/canopy interaction from above.

The floating worm rig in small-water habitat may be more productive on lunkers than other rigs. Many types of aquatic weeds hold fish and some varieties prevent a slip-sinker worm rig from working effectively. That's where the floating worm rig may come into the picture. If the weeds are within a couple of feet from the surface, this rig can produce, regardless of the bottom depth.

Some of the most fantastic strikes an angler may have happen as he plies floating worms through floating cover. Bass may explode in the middle of that stuff when the snake-like worm moves overhead. Vegetation and water sprays everywhere, and the angler may often get wet using a large near-surface worm rig.

The productive rig consists of a 12-inch long, high-buoyancy worm or plastic snake on a 4/0 Tru-Turn long-shank hook. Little or no weight is used on the rig so that it remains on the surface as it is retrieved to the boat. The weight of the worm is enough for casting purposes. The best floating worm coloration, according to some experts, is snake hue.

I prefer to use casting rigs with the floating worms. I discovered this technique several years ago and immediately noted the deadliness of the floating worm on big bass. My first catch was a seven pounder. A friend and I had put several large bass in the boat on this rig during our initial trial. The floating worm rig is a popular way to entice trophy bass from surface vegetation.

More than any other type of terrain, floating vegetation deserves a close inspection by those anglers seeking big bass. Aquatic growth is often maligned for causing problems, but it is too often responsible for a great fishery, one that is usually overlooked.

CHAPTER 15

SHINER SAVVY

The Native Baitfish Are Most Productive

EVER WATCH a live, dorsal-hooked shiner effectively work along a river bank beneath overhanging weeds and jutting limbs? Watch long enough, and you'll see an explosion at the surface as the baitfish takes to the air to escape the jaws of a giant largemouth. It's then that you may have the thrill of catching a monster bass.

The hunt, the anticipation of an immediate strike and the battle "royale" is exciting! When it gets in your blood, it is relatively easy to develop an obsession for catching huge bass on the live shiner. You're happiest with a successful manipulation of bait and the ultimate catch and release of a giant largemouth.

Many lunker bass anglers now figure that shiners are the best way to accomplish that. They're right, but there are optimal presentations for success. To amass a sizable catch of huge bass, an angler may have to rely on several methods involving shiner fishing. Prime techniques depend on the water conditions to work effectively.

The golden shiner is common to most of the country, but it's in the south where the majority of successful bait fishing methods have been developed and perfected. In states from Texas to South Carolina and as far west as California, big wall hangers averaging over ten pounds are not unusual for successful shiner fishing guides and their clients.

The live soft-rayed baitfish is an integral part of many successful techniques in southern waters because bass are believed to have a preference for it. Give the largemouth a choice between the spiny-ray bluegill and the shiner, and the silvery fish will be the one eaten most every time. Why shouldn't bass have a preference based on how edible their food might be?

Typically, native shiners go crazy when a bass of huge proportions swims by, but those grown at a shiner farm may not draw the same reaction. The wild ones just seem to trigger strikes better. Smaller, four to six-inch shiners are usually best for enticing bass action, but I'll often go with huge 10-inch long shiners. Five or six dozen shiners are normally adequate for a day's outing, using the various techniques.

An angler in the thick of things, though, can go through a lot of the baitfish. I can remember some exciting days on the water when every bass in the lake seemed to want a golden shiner, and my partner and I employed several dozen to take advantage of the concentration. A lot depends on the weather and current conditions you're fishing in and the condition of the bait, in addition to the bass activity.

If the health of the shiners is poor, they will die quickly on a hook or when placed in a strong current. As a result, most lunker bass anglers will take great care of the bait. Knowing the condition of the water in your bait well is vital to maintaining the shiners in good condition. Aerators, ice and a special granular chemical, called Catch and Release, are normally used to keep the shiners fresh and lively.

There are a couple of dozen ways to successfully catch bass on live shiners, but I feel the following methods are usually the most enjoyable and productive. 1) Anchored/Casting; 2) Drifting; 3) Anchored/Drifting Bait; 4) Motor Trolling; and 5) Wading/Casting. Selection and employment of each depends, as I've said, on the water characteristics. One of these methods will work on any given day, and often two or more may produce.

Anchor And Cast

Boat positioning and bait presentation are vital to getting continued action from a school of largemouth. Both ends of the boat should be securely anchored, and I'll usually set out three or four

A dorsal-hooked golden shiner fished beneath floating vegetation from an anchored position will often provide action. The author's largest bass, which weighed 12 1/2 pounds, was taken on the native forage.

baits, if a second person is along to assist in monitoring the rigs.

I've utilized the anchor and cast, or "dead line," technique when anchored to catch up to 25 bass. There were no real lunkers among them, but a six and one-half pounder anchored the catch, which included five others exceeding four pounds each. On another day, I caught two bass over nine pounds and on still another day, I hooked my largest ever, a 12-pounder. Many in the seven, eight and nine pound category have been caught since, and released back to their underwater sanctuary.

This method is particularly useful over submerged hydrilla in open water or under floating vegetation such as hyacinths. The southern coastal states all have the latter and hydrilla grows as far north as Illinois. I enjoy fishing patches of hydrilla, coontail moss or milfoil, all of which may grow up from the bottom and not reach the surface. An ideal spot will have one of the weed clumps about six feet off the bottom in depths of 10 or 11 feet.

During the summer and fall, this anchor and cast method is hard

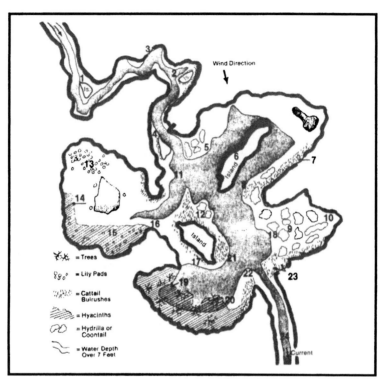

FIGURE 18 - There are two dozen potential trophy bass spots denoted on this lake. The habitat varies, and so should the shiner-fishing rig and hooking procedure. Check out the best methods to use for each spot on the next page.

to top. Fish are quite active then, and live bait can attract and hold a concentration.

Wind Drift

The drift method utilizes the wind to move the boat over submerged grass or brush flats. An angler can check out a large expanse of water with his gasoline outboard and depth flasher. Then, once he has located several potentially productive coontail or hydrilla beds, he will toss out marker buoys to pinpoint the spots with maximum weed growth. That's usually where the big bass are.

Where a noticeable drop or ledge does not occur over hydrilla, drifting is commonly used. Individual fish are normally taken from

124

Shiner Spots	Area	Technique	Rig	Hooking Procedure	Comment
1	River Island	5	2	1	Drift bait into point
2	River Fork	2	1	1	Work river side and oxbow side
3	River Bend	5	3	1	Drift bait into deep, outer bend
4	River Island	5	2	1	Work bait into bulrush point
5	Hydrilla Flats	2	1	2	Work pockets in weed bed
6	Submerged Bar	1	3	1	Troll entire length of bar
7	Rush beds	1	2	1	Work near rush edge
8	Rush Point	2	2	2	Cast all pockets and points
9	Hydrilla Flats	3	1/5	1	Drift over entire flat
10	Shallow Flat	4	4	2	Wade and cast pockets
11	Quick-drop Point	3	3	1	Drift point and sides
12	Weedy Island	1	1/5	1	Work shallows between weed beds
13	Bonnet Field	4	4/5	2	Cast all clumps and pockets
14	Floating Hyacinth	2	1	3	Fish under the cover
15	Hyacinths/Pads	2	1	3	"Run" the bait back under
16	Neck	1	2	1	Troll both sides (points)
17	Island Shallows	1	1	1	Work shallow side
18	Hydrilla Weedline	3	2	1	Drift weedline at edge
19	Hyacinths/Trees	2	3	3	Work bait in depth under cover
20	Hyacinths/Drop	2	2	3	"Run" bait back under
21	Rush Island	2	1	2	Point pockets should be worked
22	River Outlet	5	1	2	Let bait move around point
23	Rush Pockets	4	4/5	2	Work bait into all openings
24	Canal	3	3	1	Troll slowly along each bank

such areas, rather than big schools. I'll often set out three or four shiner rigs and drift through the area, pulling the bait into the prospective bass habitat. As the drift passes across bass holding spots and fish are contacted, I'll toss out marker buoys.

This method can be very successful. On some days, fish are all over the grass beds and are not concentrated in one particular spot. This method, then, is very successful and the one to use. I'll not forget an eight and one-quarter pounder that was one of three instantaneous strikes on three different rigs. It was the largest.

Anchor And Drift Bait

Where a current exists, such as in a river, this method is ideal. Springs, winds and tides can also generate water movement, and this method may be the most productive under these conditions. The boat is usually anchored up-current from the area to be fished. Anchors at each end will position the craft so that each angler can

125

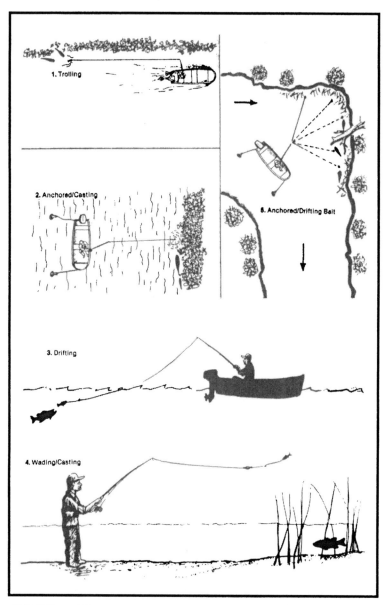

FIGURE 19 - There are several effective shiner fishing techniques that produce lunker bass. The lake or river conditions will usually determine the optimal methods to try.

126

cast his bait upstream of the hot spot. The shiners are then allowed to drift into the productive area.

Typical areas that may be fished this way include brush-filled outer bends in creeks and rivers, islands that separate current flow, weedy points on marsh tidal flats, long, wind-blown points on large lakes, etc. Wherever the current can drift your bait into an area with big bass, let it. This kind of fishing may produce results almost immediately.

I've taken several big bass out of such areas using both free-line and bobber rigs. Areas where deep water exists under a canopy of hyacinths have been especially kind to me while using this method. Several waterways offer numerous opportunities for utilizing this method. It's a fun way to fish the bait.

Troll With The Electric

In tight areas where emergent cover will hinder a straight drift, this method, utilizing an electric trolling motor to aid maneuvering, is essential. Dense bulrush or cattail weedlines with an irregular pattern may dictate use of such a method, as would, of course, certain wind strengths or direction.

I'll normally use this method to correctly place my baits along underwater ledges covered with hydrilla. Such spots often harbor concentrations of big bass. The shiner is manipulated along weedlines and into pockets in the cover that are adjacent to open water. A slight pull of the line should keep the trolled bait from burying into the vegetation. The shiner should remain next to the cover throughout the troll for maximum action.

Fresh baits which cause a lot of commotion are prime for big bass, whether trolled or cast. Let the shiner 'flutter' along the edge, six to eight inches away from the rushes, for maximum action.

Wade And Cast

Wading with boat in tow can be a refreshing way to bag bass. This method is utilized extensively in and around bulrush beds on shallow flats. The boat is usually needed to contain the supply of shiners. A seven-foot rod is particularly important for leverage when setting the hook.

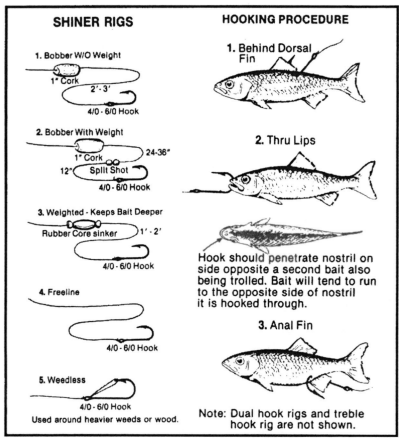

SHINER RIGS

1. Bobber W/O Weight

1" Cork

2' - 3'

4/0 - 6/0 Hook

2. Bobber With Weight

1" Cork

24-36"

12"

Split Shot

4/0 - 6/0 Hook

3. Weighted - Keeps Bait Deeper

Rubber Core sinker

1' - 2'

4/0 - 6/0 Hook

4. Freeline

4/0 - 6/0 Hook

5. Weedless

4/0 - 6/0 Hook

Used around heavier weeds or wood.

HOOKING PROCEDURE

1. Behind Dorsal Fin

2. Thru Lips

Hook should penetrate nostril on side opposite a second bait also being trolled. Bait will tend to run to the opposite side of nostril it is hooked through.

3. Anal Fin

Note: Dual hook rigs and treble hook rig are not shown.

FIGURE 20 - A good shiner fisherman may employ a variety of rigs and hooking procedures to properly present the baitfish to a trophy largemouth.

The best location for a wader to toss the shiner depends on the time of year. The pre-spawn season finds big sow bass in four or five feet of water around forage-holding cover. Bulrush beds that grow on hard bottoms and offer irregular growth patterns for the bass to ambush their prey are top spots. Post spawn activity finds the big bass in heavier cover and in a less aggressive mood. Concentrations of huge bass are more difficult to find and wade fish in the summer and fall months. Individuals can still be found in bulrush cover, however.

Once positioned about 10 yards from the fish-holding vegetation, a two-handed, smooth swing cast of the bait will be followed by an easy entry. The shiner should land softly within 12 inches of the cover. The spool is not normally engaged, since a bass would likely feel the drag and drop the shiner.

Equipment Up To The Task

Heavy seven-foot rods with plenty of hook-setting backbone and conventional level wind casting reels are normally chosen for this endeavor. Using less of a rig will hurt an angler after big bass. The giants have a knack of breaking the weakest link or not getting hooked in the first place.

Spool on anywhere from 20 to 40 pound test premium monofilament line for adequate protection against nicks and abrasions from the dense cover. Terminal tackle would include a strong 5/0 hook tied directly to the line. Variations could include a weedless hook for dense cover and a pair of split shot or small rubber-core sinkers as an additive when weight is needed to keep the shiner down. A cork can be used when needed.

The shiners can be hooked a variety of ways. Hooking one through the dorsal fin allows the baitfish maximum freedom of movement, and correspondingly, may be difficult for the angler to control around the structure being fished. Hooking a shiner through the lips is a most practical way for trolled or drifted baits, or those placed in specific locations in current where drowning would be a concern if hooked differently.

A hook through the anal fin is preferred when 'running' shiners under heavy floating cover, such as water hyacinths or water cabbage. That allows you maximum directional control. Hooking shiners through the eye sockets is a method primarily reserved for panfish anglers with small baits. Multiple hook rigs and treble hook additions are not considered practical for most fishing situations.

I've been using these rigs and presentation methods for a several years, and my catches of big bass consistently improve. Of the almost 200 largemouth that I've caught weighing being five and 13 pounds, probably one third have been enticed by a native shiner. Considering that I fish artificial lures some 90 percent of the time, that should

Regardless of the type of cover being fished, there is a productive method of fishing shiners for huge largemouth. Guide Dan Thurmond employs many, which result in bass like this.

tell you something about the effectiveness of the baitfish on big bass!

When I need a big largemouth to 'adjust' my attitude. I'll think of the favorite food fish of bass, that is, the shiner. The size of bass that I usually catch on the king-size baits puts me in a great mood. Releasing those trophies satisfy this bass angler even more!

130

CHAPTER 16

JUNGLE FLIPPIN'

Strongarm Heavy Bass In Heavy Cover

JUNGLES ARE INTIMIDATING, particularly the aquatic type. Anglers often shy away from dense, heavy cover such as bulrushes, Johnson grass, or cattails, but that is where bigger bass are found in many natural lakes. To catch your share or more, you'll have to combat the terrain.

The most productive trophy bass pattern in overwhelming habitat during the first six months of the year is flippin' the small, isolated bulrush clumps within the emergent grass. Aquatic vegetation abounds on many waters, and in such cover, the biggest bass usually hold.

During the summer heat, the best pattern for jungle bass will normally be fishing the dense buggy-whip patches or grass beds. Even in dense cover, warm-weather fish will be deeper, in five or six feet of water. Hot weather bass can be super active, and with another couple of feet of line out, may pose additional battlefield problems.

In any type of jungle terrain, points and pockets in the cover draw my attention. If unfamiliar with the water, I'll move in close to such vegetation and check the water depth and type-bottom present, prior to fishing the area. Bass prefer a clean bottom, particularly in the spring, so I look for sandy soil.

Sandy bottoms on natural lake beds encourage the growth of bulrushes. Extensive beds of the "buggy whips", as some call them, are ideal in which to flip a bait. In fact, bulrushes are preferred over cattails. Rushes are easier to fish because they are stiff and straight, and they have more underwater openings within for bass to move about.

Cattails, on the other hand, have leaves that branch off as they rise from the water's surface. Most cattail patches also grow in shallower water, and underwater, the stalks are usually too dense for a big bass to swim through. Both, however, provide jungle-type cover for smaller bass.

Not all bulrushes are the same either. The best patches of rushes, reeds or any other emergent structure can be found by eyeballing the height. The good fishing areas generally have the tallest vegetation growth due to the optimal soil conditions. Sandy bottom, for example, is extremely fertile, causing the reed jungle to grow to taller elevations.

Bass in relatively shallow waters always prefer the additional protection from "high-rise" reeds, and obviously, I prefer to place my baits where the most bass can be found. The healthiest waters have the healthiest forage base and, correspondingly, the biggest bass.

A key to catching more bass from the jungles lies in the angler's ability to observe movement. Look for any type of movement in the bulrushes or grass beds as an indicator of the presence of fish. A lot of fishermen may see movement in the vegetation and cast to it for a long time, without knowing what that fish might have been.

Where there's a large concentration of Nile perch, or tilapia as they are officially known, bass aren't usually present. The tilapia normally travel en masse and knock several stalks at once when they move. Instead of simply shaking one reed or a small clump, a tilapia will often spook and start a chain reaction.

Such bumping extravaganzas aren't indicative of bass. Largemouth are typically more curious, and they'll remain in their weed hole and just watch to see what had spooked that one fish. Likewise, seldom will an isolated fish be a member of the tilapia family...but it could be a bass. Large 'bumps' of the heavy cover are, in fact, usually largemouth bass.

Large worms can entice lunkers, like this 15 pounder, because they present at the bottom a mouthful of "forage" to the fish.

The Offerings

A pile of 8-inch black grape worms lay at my feet, and terminal tackle, consisting of a 5/0 or 6/0 Brute hook and 5/8 ounce slip sinker, is ready for the plastic imitation. Nearby, in the gunwale-attached tray lie several jigs and a couple of bottles of Berkley Strike Rind. The rind provides a little bit more bulk to slow down the fall of the jig and may attract bigger bass. Flippin' maximizes the lure's time under the surface, though, and coincidentally, it's usually in the productive strike zone!

In extremely shallow waters, I'll opt for the worm about 90 percent of the time. In dense vegetation lying in waters seven or eight feet deep, the jig-and-pork combination can be extremely effective. Either bait will work, and it depends what you're comfortably fishing.

Weed-bound bass in cold water are often sluggish and won't move fast, so a little slower-falling lure may be best. Lighten up on

133

the slip sinker or jig head size to encourage them to strike. A jig head or slip sinker weighing 3/8-ounce or less will cause the bait to fall slowly in waters below 60 degrees. That will net more strikes then, but for most conditions, you'll want to have heavier offerings.

With the heavier bait, you can cover water more quickly, but this is not a fast-moving technique. In strong winds, the heavier, fast-sinking lure will keep the bait on the bottom. On larger baits, in particular, you need to check the sharpness of the hook. It should be extremely sharp, so that it'll penetrate well.

The trailer is important to any offering in the jungle terrain. It is sometimes difficult to detect the fish, and a trailer encourages the bass to hold onto the bait longer. Since the best lure for these weed-bound bass normally resembles a crayfish, bass are used to foraging on hard, spiny morsels.

Productive lure colors to match the crustacean living in the dense habitat should be brown, black or blue/grape. The slip sinker or jig head should also be painted accordingly for best results. Match the plastic or pork additive to the head, if possible.

Effective Presentations

The real key to catching largemouth from the weedy jungles is the effective presentation of the lure. It must be smooth and quiet in these shallow environments, and timing is everything. Begin the flip by pulling off enough line with your left hand until the bait is at the water's surface. Now, raise the rod tip so that the bait lifts up off the water's surface and starts to swing toward you.

As you simultaneously strip off more line with your left hand, raise the rod tip from 10 o'clock to 12 o'clock and back. With an underhand swing, arch the lure in a pendulum motion toward the target. You can control the excess line with your left hand which should move back toward the reel, as the lure is flipped toward the cover. The left hand can also slow the lure's descent to help it drop noiselessly into the jungle.

The clump of bulrushes or other vegetation should normally be nearby, so the amount of line out at the termination of the "yo-yo" type cast is usually less than 12 feet. When flippin' in heavy cover, turn the line loose at the right moment and try to let the bait fall to the bottom directly below its ideally soft landing.

Once you have let the lure drop to the bottom on semi-limp line, you'll need to check it. Lift up on the rod lightly to determine if a fish has hit the bait while the line was slack. The key to catching jungle-bound fish is to know whether or not a bass is in possession of the lure prior to jigging it up and down.

At times, you may be wise to let the bait sit perfectly still for at least ten seconds before checking it. Then, lift the rod tip up slowly and let the lure fall back to the bottom. Now, don't move the bait for several seconds once again. Repeat the process if you still haven't had a strike. You might have to slowly "yo-yo" the bait three or four times to entice a trophy-size bass during the spring months.

"Line control is extremely important for anglers beginning to flip," notes Lakeland, Florida guide Wayne Yohn. "There's a concentration of big fish in the most dense weedbeds on natural lakes during the warmer months, and to get at them, the fisherman must be proficient at flippin'."

Experience and Proficiency

My friend and occasional fishing companion is more expert than most flippers. He's caught over 70 largemouth from the weed beds primarily on pegged slip-sinkers and plastic worms. He pulled in two largemouth over 10 pounds and several others, including a 7 pounder in a one-day Boat Tournament a couple of years ago. Yohn and his teammate amassed a 60 pound, 2 ounce stringer that day to out-fish 142 other competitors.

The 14 fish caught, mostly between noon and 2 p.m., were taken by flippin' the bulrushes. Whether in a tournament or not, Yohn believes that in the thick jungle, conventional casting methods can be a disaster. Flippin' is almost mandated in heavy terrain.

Yohn and I visited a small natural lake with the sole purpose of catching a "photo" fish. We quickly established a pattern and found that flippin' the buggy whips surrounded by thinner grass on the inside of huge beds of vegetation was most productive. It was a typical pattern for the warming spring months.

As our boat moved through acres of Johnson grass, we flipped our lures around every clump of isolated bulrushes. The fishing and breathing that warm day was tough. It seemed as though each grass stalk was the landing pad for 200 or 300 blind mosquitoes. We were inundated with thousands of them as the boat moved over the grass between clumps of bulrushes.

With absolutely no breeze to prevent the blind mosquitoes from 'clustering' about us, our flippin' probably suffered. We did, however, manage to pull in two largemouth each during the period between noon and 3 p.m. It was a slow day, but Yohn, with a deserved big bass reputation, finally caught lunkers of 6 1/2 and ten pounds even.

Technique Refinement

Yohn is a true master with the flippin' technique, and his advice is certainly worthy of note for the serious angler. He'll always recommend that anglers fish both sides of a clump of reeds. The guide has often fished one side, picked up the bait and dropped it on the other side, where a bass was waiting. Yohn has done that often enough to carve out for himself a fishing career!

In dense jungle habitats where the big bass usually are tough adversaries, Yohn prefers to let the fish mouth the baits for two or three seconds before setting the hook. If he feels a solid hit, he will, however, set back on the rod immediately. Most strikes will be of the "tap" nature though, and he'll wait a few seconds before checking to see if the bass still has it.

Bass will normally hit the bait on the initial fall, but during the first six months of the year, strikes may not be timed like that. Bass then will normally hit the lure after you have started to move it up and down.

Flippin' is probably the best technique to use when fishing the weedy jungles of natural lakes. Giant bass are waiting to be fed if you can properly present the lure to them. Hang onto those rods though!

CHAPTER 17

WHY BIG FISH GET AWAY

Mistakes Are Common, But Can Be Avoided

MANY MISTAKES CAN be made throughout the day that will cost you the trophy bass of a lifetime. It often seems too that the fish that do get away are all lunkers. Big fish have the know-how and the strength to strain the limits of our tackle, and our reflexes.

Anglers are not always prepared mentally or physically to handle a trophy fish when it strikes. They make mistakes. At other times, equipment problems limit the success of a fisherman with a big-fish opportunity. Knowing some of the potential problems to which a lunker fighter may be exposed should aid in that preparation.

Everyone makes mistakes, even the professionals. Often they are on big fish and fall into the "catastrophic error" class. Poor mental judgment is not inherent only in beginners, but it will probably show up among them more frequently.

I have fished with hundreds of anglers, from the very biggest names in tournament fishing and outdoor TV shows to total novices who had never handled a rod and reel. And, I have seen many big fish escape, even from those excellent fishermen. Some situations can't be helped, but many can.

Getting a big fish halfway to the boat only to have the hook pull out or the line snap is a frustrating experience. Hopefully, there is something to blame for loss and a bit of experience to remember. Too, the angler should learn from the mistake or failure.

Tackle to whip an 11-pound largemouth around heavy cover must be stout. Small lures need to be backed up by abrasion-resistant line.

Equipment Problems

Having sound equipment and paying proper attention to tackle details really begins on shore. Naturally, sharp hooks are a must on all natural and artificial bait offerings. Hooks pull out of big fish easily, when they are dull.

Trophy hunters often fish with big baits expressly for lunkers and their equipment should reflect that goal. Large, heavy-duty hooks are thicker than smaller ones and, thus, require sharper points and a stronger, quicker hook set. Most factory-made or installed hooks need additional sharpening.

"Whippy" rods are still responsible for many lost lunkers each year. The limber staffs of yesteryear have no place in most boats today. A medium-action rod or long, light-tip action rod should be considered the minimal stiffness acceptable to tangle with a big fish. Short rods have to overcome a leverage-deficiency in order to 'power the steel home.' Five-foot heavy action rods will surpass most problems in the hands of an experienced angler. The rod blank must

138

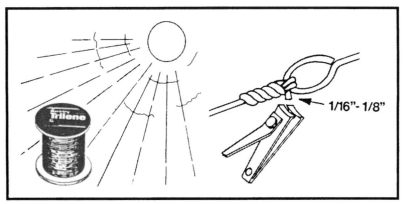

FIGURE 21 - Line is suspect when a big fish breaks off. Line left in the sun for long periods becomes weak, and the line tag end at knots when clipped too short may fail.

have adequate backbone and/or leverage to properly set the hook.

Rods that have minute fractures in them tend to come apart at the time of maximum stress, like when the lunker is powering away one last time. Broken guides also have been known to come loose or nick the line at an inappropriate time. Those are potential problems that can be eliminated at home by careful inspection.

Reel drags can be a major problem. Equipment that is old or heavily used may not have the smooth drag that is needed for handling some big fish. Too, reels that have received lots of punishment in the form of battery, grit and grime may have poorly working drags. Overhaul your gear and keep it maintained for best luck.

Improper drag setting is a common fault in the loss of big fish. Set the drag before the fish strikes, either at home or as conditions change. It should be less giving in an area of heavy timber and snags than in open water above a sand bar. Too many anglers try to adjust the drag while the fish is on. An experienced fisherman can get away with it but the average guy should not attempt it, unless the setting is off just too much.

Line is always suspect when a big fish breaks off. Line too light or too old, or an inferior knot are often the possible culprits. Going after huge fish with light pound test line is usually foolish. Naturally, the habitat and other water characteristics should dictate the line test to a certain extent.

139

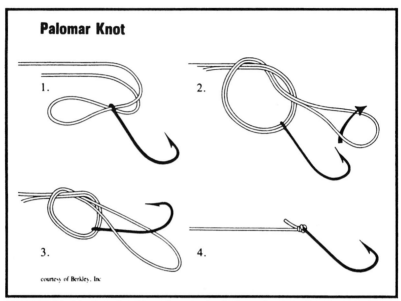

Palomar Knot

1.

2.

3.

4.

FIGURE 22 - The knot that I have found to be the best all-around knot is the Palomar. Its knot strength is almost 100 percent of the line when tied properly, and it's easier to tie than most all other knots.

Heavy cover and the potential for big bass means you should select the line suited for the job. Lines testing 14 to 20 are advisable for ten-pounders in dense weed or timber cover for example. I've often seen novice northern anglers venture south with six pound test line and light rods in hopes of doing battle with a real heavy weight. Line does have an extended shelf life, but many days in the sun or in varying temperature extremes can shorten its effectiveness severely. Repeated breaks denote either poor knot tying or rotten line. Knot tying proficiency is easily gained, but a rotten line must be replaced.

Naturally, general wear and tear can deteriorate the strength of the line too. The abrasion may not be noticeable, but the smart angler will snip off the first six feet or so of his line after each substantial use. Prevention is the best insurance against line failure and the loss of a big fish.

Terminal tackle can easily fail. Split rings, snaps, swivels or line ties can become weak or may have a manufacturing defect not noticed beforehand. Again the stress on all equipment is maximum

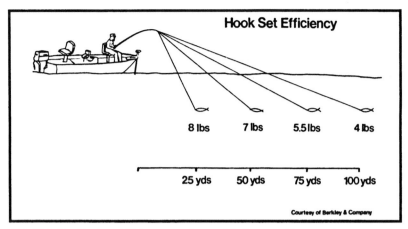

FIGURE 23 - Hook set efficiency goes down with distance. The same force exerted at the set will result in about half the force if the terminal end (lure) is 100 yards away versus 25 yards. Line stretch and friction through the water account for the difference. Use of thinner lines with minimal stretch can result in less of a difference.

when a big fish is trying to escape. Other equipment problems such as a rotten or broken net, boat seats not able to handle the strain during a battle, etc. are potential problems that should be eliminated before you get to the lake.

Physical Shortcomings

A poorly set hook is often the main cause of a big fish lost on the way to the boat. I've watched anglers fail to set the hook into a fish going away with the lure. A weak set or none due to indecision is probably the most common reason. Was it a fish or not? There's only one good way to find out - set the hook.

When fishing a plastic worm, many fishermen play a "feel game" with the fish. We've heard that the time to set the hook is just as soon as something appears different. This can be a twitch or tug on the line, or the lure coming to a halt. But, then is the time to set the hook hard!

The worm hook in most rigs has to penetrate the plastic prior to embedding in the jaw of the fish. That sounds easy until you image a plastic worm balled up inside a mouth of bone and grizzle. There

141

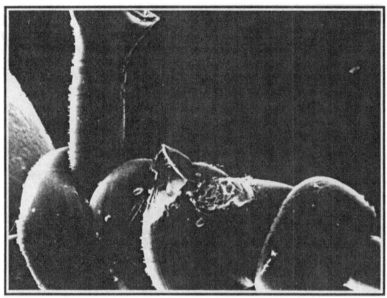

Check your line for abrasions that occur over the course of fishing around weeds or other cover. Keep in mind that even though line may look and feel undamaged, a closer look might reveal several nicks.

is little way of really telling the projection of the hook point when it will be set.

Strength and quick reflexes are the name of the game here. Even a cupped topwater lure or long-lipped crankbait will "resist" a smooth hook set. Just the resistance of the water on the plug will slow down the acceleration in a hook set. The angler that feels only a light hook set is needed for lures with exposed treble hooks is sadly mistaken. Failure to exert enough pressure to keep a big fish away from the anchor rope, outboard or trolling motor, or out of dense weeds could be the result of a physical shortcoming.

I've often seen big fish take off in heavy cover and drive so deep into it that the angler never again saw the trophy. You normally have to be in control of the fish at all times to eventually land one.

Mental Lapses

The difference between a good fisherman and a bad one is not usually the ability to think. It is the ability to apply knowledge on the water. The good angler will concentrate on what he is doing and think about what he will do if that big fish strikes his lure.

In the heat of battle, a fishing partner will occasionally grab the line to assist in the landing of a trophy. At that time, the fish has a shorter, more firm point to pull away from than a length of line running through the rod tip. It is then that most big fish get away.

Never let an inexperienced partner help you land the fish by touching your line. Net help, if effective, is great, but too much can happen on a short, taut line if the fish is still energetic. Grabbing the line to lift the lunker into the boat is dangerous indeed.

When your partner does use the net, he'll hopefully net the fish head first. Trying to net a "green" fish from the tail end is a major cause of lost trophies at boatside. If possible, for those big fish to be released after the battle, try to lip-land them. A net can cause loss of the protective slime coat and later infection on the fish.

Never try to "horse" a big fish in waters with few obstructions. That's undue strain on the equipment. Conversely, never give the fish slack line. She'll usually spit out the hook then or use the extra length to wrap around an obstruction and break the line. Both situations occur to many anglers during the heat of battle.

Knowing many of the potential causes of losing big fish, I doubt if I'll ever lose another. Ha! Want to bet?

CHAPTER 18

CATCH AND RELEASE

A Most Important Philosophy For Giant Futures

A LOT OF EMPHASIS these days is put on the catch and release of sport fish. Arguments for such personal fishery management are usually valid, particularly when talking of giant bass. Trophy largemouth are much better sport than they are food.

Fish that attain "lunker" status have been around for at least six or more years and have been doing something right to grow that large. They have either been smart enough to avoid the fake baits tossed around them or they have been living in places in which few anglers can properly present a lure. Another possibility for their longevity and growth is that they were released by conservative minded individuals.

The champion of the latter, in my mind, is Dan Thurmond. This Central Florida guide has a goal of turning back the majority of his ten-pound plus bass. The strict conservationist has a personal policy that other guides should adopt...for their future business and the enjoyment of others a few years from now. Thurmond allows only one trophy bass to be kept by a client. In fact, he's adamant about that.

A couple of years ago, Thurmond had a two-angler guide party, and they had been catching several good largemouth. The guide put the fish into the treated water as they were caught so that the largest could be determined and the rest released. Six bass between 5 and 7 3/4 pounds rested comfortably in the live well when one of the anglers said, "Looks like we'll be able to finish out our stringer."

After further discussion, Thurmond found out that the two men were looking for eight fish over five pounds each to mount on a stringer in a restaurant back in their home town.

"You're with the wrong guide to be looking for a stringer," Dan injected. "I only allow one bass per person to be taken for mounting and the rest will be turned back."

The client's mouths dropped open in shock, so Dan proceeded to tell them about another client that he had. That man had caught a bass which exceeded 11 pounds and just 15 minutes later had caught a 12 pounder. Thurmond looked down at the second fish and told him, "Well, you've got your choice. You can have the 11 or the 12. One of them is going back."

"No way, I want both of them," said the client. "I'm paying you, and I want them both."

After talking to him a few more minutes, Thurmond saw that he wasn't getting anywhere. So, he just decided to put them both back and they'd go on in and quit for the day. And they did, recounted Thurmond.

Thurmond looked at the biggest of the two-man party, a 250 pounder, and said, "And you know what, that guy was bigger than you!"

The two quickly decided then that they would continue fishing, and that they would put the smaller bass back, keep the two seven-pounders and hope for a bigger fish. If they didn't find one they would be satisfied with those two. Thurmond reported the three of them having a good time for the rest of that day.

The guide believes that his attitude towards conservation of the outsize bass are the reasons for him and his clients' success at catching over 400 ten-pound plus largemouth. His dedication to those principles go far. On his birthday a couple of years ago, he and a friend fished together. They left his house early, at 4 a.m., to get to a favorite spot on a nearby lake.

They anchored the boat there, and then when the sun was getting up to where they could barely see the cover 50 feet away, Dan noticed that their boat was not positioned on the spot properly. They re-anchored and were soon sitting there with the live shiners

Releasing a 16-pound largemouth takes a lot of will power. Releasing the smaller 10 and 12 pounders takes foresight. If we don't, there won't be any 16 pounders to catch two or three years later.

cruising the weed fringes. Within a couple of minutes, a big fish hit one of the baits.

"That's a good fish," Dan told his friend. "You want it?"

"No, it's your birthday. You go ahead," the friend replied, so Dan reeled up the slack and set the hook. The fish came completely out of the water twice but was soon landed.

"Oh, I'm sorry! it's over 12 pounds! You have not caught one over 12, and if I'd known, you would have had it," he apologized.

Upon close inspection, they noticed that the 12 pound, 4 ounce fish had one of their tags already in it. Dan often weighs and tags his big bass prior to release.

About 45 minutes later, his friend noticed another cork disappear. The hook was set, and the huge largemouth was eventually worked to the net. Like Dan's big bass, his friend's 13 pound, 4 ounce sow was also put right back in the lake. They fished five or ten minutes more and left when the first boats started coming in.

When Thurmond had started guiding clients on the lake in early January, there were few other boats even fishing it. But once the word got out that he was getting some fish, pressure increased substantially. That makes it even more important to release the big fish, according to the guide.

Thurmond caught his first big fish there on January 25 and, in the following two months, caught 13 more bass over 10 pounds from that very spot. Nine of those fish were released right in that same place. The guide has released other 13 pounders, but the three biggest pulled over his gunwale were kept. Thurmond acknowledges that it's just difficult to get clients to release those that weigh between 14 and 16 pounds!

Spawning Considerations

During the spawning season, trophy bass can be caught off the beds, if you are persistent. The bass normally has to be teased into taking a bait, whether natural or artificial. It may take a 100 casts or even more to provoke a bass to remove a lure from the immediate area. An angler may have to drag his bait over the bed numerous times and watch the fish move in and out of the bed area over several hours, before catching that fish. Eventually, that fish will take the bait, leaving another bed vacant.

Is bed fishing ethical, sporting or really wise in our world today? Many big bass researchers believe that removal of a trophy size fish on their beds (or later) depletes the gene pool. In other words, the giants and their potential offspring (with the genetic makeup to grow to such proportions) are eliminated from the fishery. The spawn pool remaining is little bass and the resulting overall population will be progressively smaller fish.

Other biologists say that there is no biological evidence that catches during the spawn have an adverse impact on the bass fishery. Habitat, rather than fishing pressure during this time of year determines the bass population, some believe. In heavily fished waters, this is a time that anglers can wreck havoc on the bass population, according to Bob Knopf, a former biologist. He has used scuba to observe this in the aquatic environment and believes that the result can be an extremely poor bass fishery for a few years.

"Even if you fish the male bass then, you can destroy the spawn," says the underwater researcher. "If you catch the male bass off that

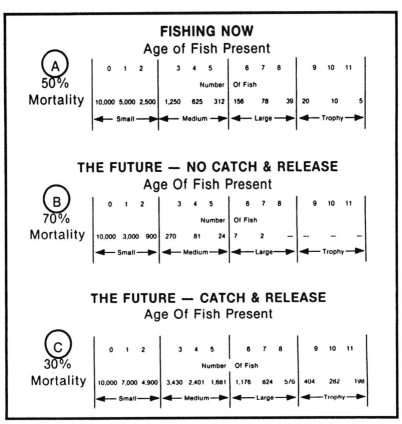

FIGURE 24 - *Look at Chart A which is a typical bass population in a moderately-fished lake (assuming a 50 percent mortality). Notice the numbers of trophy fish (nine pounds and up). A lake with heavy fishing pressure would have a population base like that shown in Chart B. That assumes a corresponding 70 percent mortality and that catch and release is not followed. In Chart C, the trophy bass population is significantly greater, thanks to catch and release management practices and the resulting mortality rate of 30 percent. Unfortunately, many lakes across the country are represented by Chart B. Which population do you want in our future?*

bed, even though you might release him quickly and he swims back to the nest, the bluegills are eating the eggs as you are doing all of that. A lot of times, though, the bass will not go right back to the nest. He'll drop right off that edge and stay in that slightly deeper channel for an hour or so. When he comes back in to the nest, it could be destroyed by then."

Trophy size bass are more aggressive than usual during this time, and they are more vulnerable to the angler since they are in shallow water. Their senses are fine tuned during the spawn, but they put their lives in jeopardy by moving shallow. Roe-laden bass on the bed offers an angler a good opportunity to catch a lunker, but you don't have to kill it.

Taking bass from the beds after the eggs have been laid or the fry have been hatched, is not much sport. Both sexes of fish are in their poorest condition of the year.

Trophy Regulation Readiness

The angling public appears to be ready for stricter regulations and better management of the trophy bass resource. In a survey of 1986 license holders, the Florida Game and Fresh Water Fish Commission found that approximately two-thirds of the respondents favored a reduced bag limit for largemouth. The same number favored a program whereby water bodies would be selected specifically for trophy bass management.

Furthermore, the majority of anglers stated they would be willing to drive over 50 miles to fish in a trophy lake, even if it had a limit of one bass over six pounds. Anglers today prefer to catch larger bass. In fact, only one out of every six angler respondents preferred to catch a limit of 10 one-pounders versus just a couple of larger bass. The vast majority approved of "Catch-and-Release" fishing.

From the results, it is apparent that 83 percent of the anglers would be satisfied with a slot limit imposed on such trophy waters. A 14- to 21-inch slot on most lakes in the state would allow an angler an opportunity to catch and release two or three bass within that slot and grow several largemouth that would top 21 inches.

Given that data, what is being done about enhancing the trophy bass fishery in Florida? The Game and Fresh Water Fish Commission is doing some test projects on mostly small bodies of water, but they have yet to develop a serious program toward satisfying the majority of anglers. Until, they get in gear, it will be up to individuals to protect the trophy bass resource.

APPENDIX A
STATE-BY-STATE LARGEMOUTH RECORDS

STATE	WT.(lb.-oz.)	LOCATION	DATE
Alabama	16 - 8	Mountain View Lake	1987
Arizona	14 - 2	Roosevelt Lake	1956
Arkansas	16 - 4	Lake Mallard	1976
California	21 - 3 1/5	Lake Casitas	1980
Colorado	10 - 6 1/4	Stalker Lake	1979
Connecticut	12 - 14	Mashapaug Lake	1961
Delaware	10 - 5	Andrews Lake	1980
Florida	20 - 2	Big Fish Lake	1923
Georgia	22 - 4	Montgomery Lake	1932
Hawaii	8 - 0	Kilauea, Kauai	1978
Idaho	10 - 15	Anderson Lake	Unkn
Illinois	13 - 1	Stone Quarry Lake	1976
Indiana	11 - 11	Ferdinand Reservoir	1968
Iowa	10 - 12	Lake Fisher	1984
Kansas	11 - 12	Farm Pond	1977
Kentucky	13 - 10 1/4	Woods Creek Lake	1984
Louisiana	12 - 0	Farm Pond	1975
Maine	11 - 10	Moose Pond	1968
Maryland	11 - 2	Farm Pond	1983
Massachusetts	15 - 8	Sampson's Pond	1975
Michigan	11 - 15	Big Pine Is. Lake	1934
Minnesota	9 - 9 1/2	Fountain Lake	1986
Mississippi	14 - 2	Tippah County Lake	1987
Missouri	13 - 14	Bull Shoals	1961
Montana	8 - 2 1/2	Milnor Lake	1984
Nebraska	10 - 11	Sandpit	1965
Nevada	11 - 0	Lake Mohave	1972
New Hampshire	10 - 8	Lake Potanipo	1967
New Jersey	10 - 14	Menantico Pond	1980
New Mexico	11 - 0	Ute Lake	1975
New York	11 - 4 1/6	Buckhorn Lake	1987
North Carolina	14 - 15	Santeetlah Reservoir	1963
North Dakota	8 - 7 1/2	Nelson Lake	1983
Ohio	13 - 2	Farm Pond	1976
Oklahoma	12 - 13	Lake Fuqua	1989
Oregon	11 - 0	McKay Reservoir	1985

STATE	WT.(lb.-oz.)	LOCATION	DATE
Pennsylvania	11 - 3	Birch Run Reservoir	1983
Rhode Island	10 - 5	Wordens Pond	1987
South Carolina	16 - 2	Lake Marion	1949
South Dakota	8 - 14	Jackson Co. Pond	1986
Tennessee	14 - 8	Sugar Creek	1954
Texas	17 - 10 3/4	Lake Fork	1986
Utah	10 - 2	Lake Powell	1974
Vermont	9 - 11	Connecticut River	1986
Virginia	16 - 4	Lake Conners	1985
Washington	11 - 9	Banks Lake	1977
West Virginia	10 - 13	Sleepy Creek Lake	1979
Wisconsin	11 - 3	Lake Ripley	1940
Wyoming	7 - 2	Stove Lake	1942

Please Note: the above figures will be constantly changing. Each year, one to four new state records are generally set. Check with your local fish and game agency for the latest mark on the books.

Photo/Figure Credits

(Page No.-Name)

2-Jimmy Brunson; 7-Darcy Coppage; 13-Phil Binks; 19-Paul Shaffler; 20-Stan Kirkland; 21-Bud LaRoche; 24-Missouri Department of Conservation; 42-John Fitzhugh; 44, Fig. 21, 22, 23, 24-Berkley & Co.

APPENDIX B
OFFICIAL 1989 WORLD RECORDS
(Courtesy of the Fishing Hall of Fame)

Line Class	Lbs.-Ozs.	Angler	Where Caught	Date
BASS, Largemouth (Micropterus salmoides)				
All Tackle	22-4	George W. Perry	Montgomery Lake, Georgia, USA	6-2-32
Division #1—Rod/Reel				
2 lb.	6-11	Les Imler	Lake Henshaw, California, USA	6-1-85
4 lb.	15-9	Richard King	Castaic Lake, California, USA	9-21-85
6 lb.	16-0	Chuck Strauss	Castaic Lake, California, USA	7-8-83
8 lb.	21-3	Raymond D. Easley	Lake Casitas, California, USA	3-4-80
10 lb.	16-9	Stephen P. Merlo	Isabella Reservoir, California, USA	10-1-83
12 lb.	19-3	Arden Charles Hanline	Morena Lake, California, USA	2-15-87
14 lb.	13-11	Lee Hodges	Cobb Pond, Georgia, USA	7-21-87
15 lb.	19-1	Sandra W. DeFresco	Miramar Lake, California, USA	3-14-88
16 lb.	14-3	Gregory A. Tucker	Aliceville Lake, Alabama, USA	1-7-89
17 lb.	16-12	David R. Presley	Chatuge Lake, Georgia, USA	3-27-76
20 lb.	12-6	Lex Witt	Lake Humphrey's, Oklahoma, USA	10-26-87
25 lb.	15-7	Evan Brock	Johns Lake, Florida, USA	1-1-89
30 lb.	16-2	Joseph Smiley	St. Johns River, Florida, USA	1-7-83
Unlimited	16-3	Henry C. Daniel, Jr.	Ocala Nat'l. Forest, Florida, USA	2-7-76

Division #2—Fly Fishing

Class	Weight	Angler	Location	Date
2 lb.	6-8	Donnie Thomas	Eden Pond, North Carolina, USA	5-30-85
4 lb.	8-8	Ronald H. McMillian, Sr.	Clarks Hill Lake, Georgia, USA	6-2-85
6 lb.	8-0	Earl Mitchell	Hampton Lake, Florida, USA	9-24-77
8 lb.	8-1	George Chittum III	Patterson Creek, West Virginia, USA	4-11-87
10 lb.	6-0	William T. Paul	Palm River, Florida, USA	3-27-82
12 lb.	2-0	James Swinehart	Hillsdale Lake, Kansas, USA	6-26-88
14 lb.	3-1	Donald O. King	Hillsdale Lake, Kansas, USA	6-4-88
16 lb.	OPEN			
Unlimited	12-4	James W. Stone	Valentine Pond, Georgia, USA	6-30-84

Division #3—Pole/Line/No Reel

Class	Weight	Angler	Location	Date
Heaviest (only)	15-2	Harry H. Woods	Port Afields, Florida, USA	2-1-86

Division #4—Ice Fishing

Class	Weight	Angler	Location	Date
Heaviest Pole/Line	9-0	Ted Moose	Davies Lake, Illinois, USA	1-10-88
Heaviest Tip-Up	9-0	Ronald Kutilek	Plainfield Strip Pit, Illinois, USA	2-2-86

World Record Keeping Agencies
(Line-Class and All-Tackle)

1. National Freshwater Fishing Hall of Fame, Box 33, Hall of Fame Drive, Hayward, Wisconsin 54843, telephone (715) 634-4440
2. International Game Fish Association, 3000 E. Las Olas Blvd., Ft. Lauderdale, FL 33316, telephone (305) 467-0161.

BASS SERIES LIBRARY!

Eight Great Books With A Wealth Of Information For Bass Fishermen

By Larry Larsen

I. FOLLOW THE FORAGE FOR BETTER BASS ANGLING - VOLUME 1 BASS/ PREY RELATIONSHIP - The most important key to catching bass is finding them in a feeding mood. Knowing the predominant forage, its activity and availability, as well as its location in a body of water will enable an angler to catch more and larger bass. Whether you fish artificial lures or live bait, you will benefit from this book.

SPECIAL FEATURES   o PREDATOR/FORAGE INTERACTION
    o BASS FEEDING BEHAVIOR
    o UNDERSTANDING BASS FORAGE
    o BASS/PREY PREFERENCES
    o FORAGE ACTIVITY CHART

II. FOLLOW THE FORAGE FOR BETTER BASS ANGLING - VOLUME 2 TECH-NIQUES - Beginners and veterans alike will achieve more success utilizing proven concepts that are based on predator/forage interactions. Understanding the reasons behind lure or bait success will result in highly productive, bass-catching patterns.

SPECIAL FEATURES   o LURE SELECTION CRITERIA
    o EFFECTIVE PATTERN DEVELOPMENT
    o NEW BASS CATCHING TACTICS
    o FORAGING HABITAT
    o BAIT AND LURE METHODS

III. BASS PRO STRATEGIES - Professional fishermen have opportunities to devote extended amounts of time to analyzing a body of water and planning a productive day on it. They know how changes in pH, water temperature, color and fluctuations affect bass fishing, and they know how to adapt to weather and topographical variations. This book reveals the methods that the country's most successful tournament anglers have employed to catch bass almost every time out. The reader's productivity should improve after spending a few hours with this compilation of techniques!

SPECIAL FEATURES   o MAPPING & WATER ELIMINATION
                                     o LOCATE DEEP & SHALLOW BASS
                                     o BOAT POSITION FACTORS
                                     o WATER CHEMISTRY INFLUENCES
                                     o WEATHER EFFECTS
                                     o TOPOGRAPHICAL TECHNIQUES

IV. BASS LURES - TRICKS & TECHNIQUES - Modifications of lures and development of new baits and techniques continue to keep the fare fresh, and that's important. Bass seem to become "accustomed" to the same artificials and presentations seen over and over again. As a result, they become harder to catch. It's the new approach that again sparks the interest of some largemouth. To that end, this book explores some of the latest ideas for modifying, rigging and using them. The lure modifications, tricks and techniques presented within these covers will work anywhere in the country.

SPECIAL FEATURES   o UNIQUE LURE MODIFICATIONS
                                     o IN-DEPTH VARIABLE REASONING
                                     o PRODUCTIVE PRESENTATIONS
                                     o EFFECTIVE NEW RIGGINGS
                                     o TECHNOLOGICAL ADVANCES

V. SHALLOW WATER BASS - Catching shallow water largemouth is not particularly difficult. Catching lots of them usually is. Even more challenging is catching lunker-size bass in seasons other than during the spring spawn. Anglers applying the information within the covers of this book on marshes, estuaries, reservoirs, lakes, creeks or small ponds should triple their results. The book details productive new tactics to apply to thin-water angling. Numerous photographs and figures easily define the optimal locations and proven methods to catch bass.

SPECIAL FEATURES   o UNDERSTANDING BASS/COVER INTERFACE
                                     o METHODS TO LOCATE BASS CONCENTRATIONS
                                     o ANALYSIS OF WATER TYPES
                                     o TACTICS FOR SPECIFIC HABITATS
                                     o LARSEN'S "FLORA FACTOR"

VI. BASS FISHING FACTS - This angler's guide to the lifestyles and behavior of the black bass is a reference source of sorts, never before compiled. The book explores the behavior of bass during pre- and post-spawn as well as during bedding season. It examines how bass utilize their senses to feed and how they respond to environmental factors. The book details how fishermen can be more productive by applying such knowledge to their bass angling. The information within the covers of this book includes those bass species, known as "other" bass, such as redeye, Suwannee, spotted, etc.

SPECIAL FEATURES   o BASS FORAGING MOTIVATORS
                                     o DETAILED SPRING MOVEMENTS
                                     o A LOOK AT BASS SENSES
                                     o GENETIC INTRODUCTION/STUDIES
                                     o MINOR BASS SPECIES & HABITATS

VII. TROPHY BASS - is focused at today's dedicated lunker hunters who find more enjoyment in wrestling with one or two monster largemouth than with a "panfull" of yearlings. To help the reader better understand how to catch big bass, a majority of this book explores productive techniques for trophies. The "how to" information was gleaned from professional guides and other experienced trophy bass hunters. This book takes a look at the geographical areas and waters that offer better opportunities to catch giant bass.

SPECIAL FEATURES   o GEOGRAPHIC DISTRIBUTIONS
                                o STATE RECORD INFORMATION
                                o GENETIC GIANTS
                                o TECHNIQUES FOR TROPHIES
                                o LOCATION CONSIDERATIONS
                                o LURE AND BAIT TIMING

VIII. AN ANGLER'S GUIDE TO BASS PATTERNS examines the most effective combination of lure, method and places. Being able to develop a pattern of successful methods and lures for specific habitats and environmental conditions is the key to catching several bass on each fishing trip. Understanding bass movements and activities and the most appropriate and effective techniques to employ will add many pounds of enjoyment to the sport of bass fishing. "Bass Patterns" is a reference source for all anglers, regardless of where they live or their skill level.

SPECIAL FEATURES   o BOAT POSITIONING
                                o NEW WATER STRATEGIES
                                o DEPTH AND COVER CONCEPTS
                                o MOVING WATER TACTICS
                                o WEATHER/ACTIVITY FACTORS
                                o TRANSITIONAL TECHNIQUES

Breinigsville, PA USA
25 June 2010
240552BV00004B/7/P

9 780936 513065